PRACTICAL GARDENING HANDBOOK

houseplants

PRACTICAL GARDENING HANDBOOK

houseplants

PETER McHoy

LORENZ BOOKS

This edition published by Lorenz Books in 2002

© Anness Publishing Limited 1994, 2000, 2002

Lorenz Books is an imprint of Anness Publishing Limited
Hermes House, 88–89 Blackfriars Road, London SE1 8HA

Published in the USA by Lorenz Books, Anness Publishing Inc.
27 West 20th Street, New York, NY 10011

www.lorenzbooks.com

This edition distributed in Canada by Raincoast Books
9050 Shaughnessy Street, Vancouver, British Columbia V6P 6E5

A CIP catalogue record for this book is available
from the British Library.

Publisher: Joanna Lorenz
Project Editors: Judith Simons and
 Clare Nicholson
Designer: Peter Butler
Photographer: John Freeman
Illustrator: King & King Associates

Previously published as *The Houseplant Care Manual*

10 9 8 7 6 5 4 3 2 1

Contents

Introduction

Some use houseplants purely as decorations, like ornaments or paintings on the wall, others treat them almost as botanical specimens, choosing examples of the native flora from every continent. However, if you want to get the best out of your houseplants, you need to appreciate them as plants as well as decorations and some understanding of the different plant groups will help you to display them appropriately and grow them more successfully. In the first chapter, *Discovering Houseplants*, you will find advice on how to recognize and use all the major plant groups around the home, along with tips on selecting the best plants for different positions.

However, be prepared to experiment with plants, accept that there will be failures, and look beyond the commonplace to discover the range of interesting or more unusual plants that you can grow in the home. Growing houseplants will then become an even more stimulating hobby.

The second chapter, *Caring for Houseplants*, will give you the advice and guidance you need to keep your plants in tip-top condition. Houseplants do, of course, demand time and attention. If you forget to water them, few will forgive the lapse. If you don't feed them, most will look weak and starved. None of this should deter anyone from growing them, for there are always plants and techniques that you can choose to suit the time you can devote to your plants.

For example, if watering is something you just can't remember to think about every day, or business or pleasure travel takes you away from home and there's nobody to plant-sit for you, there are simple solutions: concentrate on cacti and succulents that are naturally adapted to this kind of deprivation, or grow ordinary houseplants in special containers. Self-watering planters are ideal for groups of plants and you only need to top up the reservoir every week or so. Hydro-culture is another excellent option if you want to minimize the watering chore. Feeding is also easy with modern fertilizers. There are slow-release tablets and sticks that you can push into the compost (potting soil) to release nutrients over a long period.

All these aids for the busy person are extremely useful, but caring for your plants can be a pleasurable part of growing them. By grooming them occasionally you not only notice whether pests are about to launch an attack, you also get to know your plants better, and often you will see things that would otherwise go unnoticed. If you do no more than slosh a bit of water onto your aspidistra you will soon take it for granted. But if you groom it by removing a dying leaf, or wiping the leaves over with a moist cloth to bring back the sparkle and gloss, you may suddenly notice a curious-looking purple flower sitting at compost level, a gem that you would otherwise miss. Houseplants are full of surprises, many of which only reveal themselves when you *really* care for them.

OPPOSITE: *A large specimen plant, such as this majestic palm, will make a statement in any home.*

RIGHT: *Plant groupings, such as these ferns displayed in a basket, create a stronger visual impact than single plants dotted around a room.*

Raising your own houseplants from seeds or cuttings can be extremely rewarding, and the third chapter, *Simple Multiplication*, offers clear advice on a whole range of different propagation techniques. Most houseplants can be raised from simple cuttings but, unlike hardy plants, the majority require warmth and humidity to root rapidly, so a propagator is a good investment. Apart from its use for cuttings, it will enable a whole range of seedlings to be started off in spring for both home and garden.

Lack of a propagator is only a restriction and not a bar to successful propagation. Seeds can be germinated in any warm location (provided that they are moved into a light position *without delay* as soon as the first ones have germinated). You can make a mini propagator by covering a pot with a clear plastic bag. Alternatively, a sheet of glass placed over a seed tray or a small cardboard box containing cuttings, can often work wonders with quite tricky plants.

Some people find propagation so fascinating that it becomes a hobby itself – with a constant search for new plants to try from cuttings or seed. Friends and neighbours are usually happy to spare a shoot or leaf from a plant that you take a fancy to, and looking through the seed catalogues for interesting houseplants to try is a pleasurable pastime.

Chapter 4, *Trouble-shooting*, is devoted to the problems you may experience in caring for your houseplants. Pests and diseases will undoubtedly occur from time to time. However, it should not be necessary to reach for potent sprays or to take drastic action such as discarding your plants as a first step. If a watch is kept for early signs of trouble when you groom the plants on a regular basis, pests like aphids can be eliminated before they breed and multiply. For example,

ABOVE: *Nurseries and garden centres often offer a good selection of the more popular houseplants and some specialize in particular plants such as cacti and succulents .*

BELOW LEFT: *Collecting cacti and succulents can be a fascinating hobby. The examples shown here are, from left to right:* Echinocactus grusonii, Euphorbia milii *(syn.* E. splendens*) and* Opuntia vestita.

OPPOSITE LEFT: *Some plants, such as* codiaeums, *can be quite difficult to rear, but the challenge is worth pursuing.*

OPPOSITE RIGHT: *Bathrooms can be quite tricky locations for many plants, so be sure to select those that enjoy humidity.*

many leaf diseases can be contained or eliminated simply by picking off any affected parts as soon as the disease is noticed. This will often prevent the disease from spreading and, more importantly, from releasing spores that will affect other parts of the plant or its neighbours.

While fast action is commendable, the overkill approach that resorts to a chemical armoury first is not always appropriate. If you want to avoid the use of chemicals completely, you can try a combination of good hygiene, vigilant hand picking and natural

predators. You can buy predatory insects that parasitize pests such as whitefly, and although intended for use primarily in the greenhouse can be used indoors. They are useful in a conservatory, but natural control is not without problems: you have to accept a low level of pest infestation otherwise the predator dies out, and if you try to knock out the insects not controlled by the predator using insecticides that kill a broad range of pests, you will again upset the natural control cycle.

Sometimes plants fall sick for other reasons, such as nutritional deficiencies or physiological reasons. Plants that are pot-bound will look sick, and even too much feeding will cause symptoms of collapse that could be mistaken for pests or diseases affecting the roots.

In the final chapter, *Creative Displays*, you will find lots of ideas for using houseplants imaginatively, with suggestions for different rooms, and for ways in which you can use plants together so that one enhances the other. By using houseplants as ornaments, focal points and as integrated decorations in the home, you will derive even more pleasure from your plants than you would by regarding them merely as botanical specimens.

Although plants are constantly changing – they grow, die, or simply alter their shape – this very lack of stability can be turned to your advantage. Unlike any other decorative element that you can place and forget, and eventually even take for granted, plants have a dynamic existence. You have to move them, rearrange them, even repot them into different containers, all of which gives them an extra dimension and vitality that other kinds of ornaments lack. Flowering plants usually make a transient impact, but their use in internal design is no less powerful than that of the aristocratic yucca or tall ficus. You can choose flowers and backgrounds that

blend or contrast, to complement the mood you are trying to create.

Plants not only need to look good in a setting, they have to be happy there too. No matter how grand a plant looks in a rather gloomy corner of the room, it won't thrive, or even survive, if it needs good light. Plants that demand a humid atmosphere might survive in a kitchen but not in a living-room.

The creative displays used here should provide plenty of inspiration, but be prepared to experiment with your own ideas, to suit *your* tastes and *your* home. Above all, houseplants should please you and express your own personal tastes.

Discovering houseplants

GROWING HOUSEPLANTS SHOULD BE A VOYAGE OF DISCOVERY, NOT ONLY ABOUT THE TYPES OF PLANTS THAT WILL OR WON'T GROW WELL IN YOUR HOME, BUT ALSO AN EXPLORATION OF THE PLANT KINGDOM IN ALL ITS DIVERSE MANIFESTATIONS. YOU WILL GET A LOT MORE OUT OF YOUR HOUSE-PLANTS IF YOU INVESTIGATE THE POTENTIAL OF THE VARIOUS TYPES OF PLANTS, AND HOW THEY CAN BE USED IN THE HOME.

Dependable evergreens

CHOOSE SOME OF THE EASIEST AND MOST DEPENDABLE EVERGREENS AS THE
BACKBONE OF YOUR DISPLAYS. MANY OF THEM ARE TOUGH ENOUGH FOR
THE MORE DIFFICULT POSITIONS AROUND THE HOME, AND MOST OF THOSE
SUGGESTED HERE ARE BOLD ENOUGH TO BE FOCAL POINT PLANTS TOO.

The glossy evergreens such as dracaenas, fatsias, ficus, scheffleras, palms and philodendrons generally make excellent stand-alone plants, but they can also be used as the framework plants for groups and arrangements. They will be far more robust than plants with thin or papery leaves, feathery and frondy ferns, or even those with hairy leaves. You need these other leaf textures, as well as flowering plants, to add variety of shape and form, and a touch of colour, but it makes sense to use the toughest evergreens as the basis of your houseplant displays.

Indoor 'trees'
Even the plainest room can be brought to life and given a sense of design and character with a large specimen plant that has the stature of a small tree. Some houseplants grow into real trees in their natural environment, but indoors you need plants that are in proportion with the dimensions of your room, and that won't quickly outgrow their space.

Large palms are ideal for this purpose, but many of the ficus family do just as well. The common *Ficus elastica*, once so popular, but now often passed by as unexciting, is a good choice, and there are many excellent variegated varieties that are far from dull. If you want an all-green one (and these have the merit of growing more quickly than the variegated kinds), 'Robusta' is a good variety to choose. If you don't like the upright and

TOP: Ficus elastica *was once a very popular houseplant, and is still well worth growing. The variety usually grown is 'Robusta', an improvement on the species that used to be grown years ago.*

ABOVE: Ficus lyrata *is a bold 'architectural' plant that can easily reach ceiling height.*

FAR LEFT: Philodendron scandens *is effective both as a trailing plant and grown up a moss pole, as here.*

LEFT: Yucca elephantipes *is a justifiably popular houseplant. It makes a bold focal point and is a really tough plant that should survive for years.*

metimes leggy appearance of this
ant, cut out the tip when it is about
5–1.8m (5–6ft) feet high, to stimu-
te low branching.

Other ficus to look for are *F. lyrata*
ery large leaves with a distinctive
ape), *F. benghalensis* (though the
owny appearance of the leaves can
ake it a dull-looking plant), and the
idely available *Ficus benjamina*. This
especially beautiful because it
rows tall with a broad crown and
ching branches. There are also
eautiful variegated varieties of this
ecies such as 'Starlight'.

Bushy plants that will give height
nd spread include *Schefflera arboricola*
yn. *Heptapleurum arboricola*) and
hefflera actinophylla*. Both have
nger-like leaflets radiating from a
entral point.

hen a tough plant is needed

you need a tough, glossy evergreen
r a cold or draughty spot, perhaps for
hallway or near the back door, con-
der using some of the hardy foliage
ants that have to cope with frost and
ales when planted outdoors!

Fatsia japonica is another glossy
vergreen with fingered foliage,
ather like the palm of a hand (look
r a variegated variety if you don't

like the plain green leaves). Closely
related is × *Fatshedera lizei*, a
bigeneric hybrid between *Fatsia japonica* and an ivy. Grow it as a shrub by
pinching out the growing tips each
spring, or let it show its ivy parentage
and grow more upright.

Others to look for are variegated
varieties of *Aucuba japonica*, and *Euonymus japonicus* varieties such as
'Mediopictus', 'Microphyllus Albo-
variegatus' and 'Microphyllus Aureo-
variegatus'.

Ivies are ideal if you need a tough
climber or trailer, and there are lots of
varieties to choose from, with a wide
choice of leaf shape, size and colour.

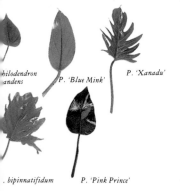

*hilodendron
andens   P. 'Blue Mink'   P. 'Xanadu'

*. bipinnatifidum   P. 'Pink Prince'

hilodendron leaves

ome genera have species and varieties with
ery different leaves, and they can make an
nteresting collection. The five philodendron
eaves shown here are typical of the variation
ou can find within one group of plants.

TOP RIGHT: Monstera deliciosa *is one of
the most striking focal point foliage plants
that you can grow. The leaves are big and
shapely, and the plant will grow large.*

ABOVE: Scindapsus aureus, *often sold
under its other name of* Epipremnum
aureum, *is a useful climber or trailer. This
is the golden variety 'Neon'.*

ABOVE RIGHT: *Radermachera combines
tough, glossy leaves with a 'loose' and almost
ferny appearance; a refreshing change to most
of the glossy evergreens.*

RIGHT: Aspidistra elatior *is a tough plant
that seems to tolerate all kinds of neglect. If
you look after it properly, however, you will
have a fine foliage plant. There is also a
variegated variety.*

Elegant palms

PALMS ARE THE EPITOME OF ELEGANCE AND WILL ADD A TOUCH OF SOPHIS-
TICATION TO YOUR HOME. THEY BRING TO MIND IMAGES OF A TINKLING
PIANO IN THE PALM COURT OF A GRAND HOTEL, YET SOME CAN LOOK JUST AS
ELEGANT AND IMPOSING IN AN ULTRA-MODERN HOME INTERIOR.

Many palms are slow-growing, and, consequently, large specimens are often expensive. But don't be deterred from trying palms; if you provide the right conditions, even small plants will gradually become impressive specimens.

Not all palms grow large, and many are compact enough for a table-top or for pride of place on a pedestal. Some are even small enough to use in a bottle garden while young. The box opposite will help you choose a suitable palm for a particular position.

How to grow healthy palms

The most common mistake is to re-gard all palms as lovers of hot sunshine and desert-dry air. They often have to cope with both in countries where they grow outdoors, but as houseplants you want them to remain in good condition with unblemished leaves.

- Keep cool in winter, but not less than 10°C (50°F).
- Keep out of direct sunshine unless you know that your palm revels in sunshine (a few do).
- Use a loam-based compost (potting soil) and ensure that the drainage is good (poor drainage is sure to cause problems).
- Only repot when absolutely essential as palms dislike root disturbance. Always ensure that the new compost is firmly compacted if you do repot.
- Water liberally in spring and summer, sparingly in winter.
- Mist the plants frequently with water and sponge the leaves occasionally with water.
- Do not use an aerosol leaf shine.

WHAT WENT WRONG

🐛 **Brown leaf tips** are usually caused by dry air. Underwatering and cold are other likely causes.

🐛 **Brown spots on the leaves** are probably caused by a disease, encouraged by overwatering or chills. Cut off all affected leaves.

🐛 **Yellowing leaves** are most likely to be caused by underwatering, though they could also indicate that the plant needs feeding.

🐛 **Brown leaves** are nothing to worry about if they are few in number and only the lowest ones are affected.

LEFT: *Washingtonia palms have fan-like leaves that create a striking effect.*

CHOOSING A PALM

Tall and tough

Chamaerops humilis Can be grown outdoors where frosts are only mild; suitable for a cold position indoors. *Howeia forsteriana* (syn. *Kentia forsteriana*) and *H. belmoreana* (syn. *K. belmoreana*) Associated with the old palm courts. Will survive in a dark situation, but growth is very slow. *Phoenix canariensis* This one enjoys full sun (but beware of leaf scorch through glass) and can sit on the patio for the summer. Keep in a cool room – minimum about 7°C(45°F) – in winter.

Table-top and easy

Chamaedorea elegans (syn. *Neanthe bella*) Can be used in a bottle garden when small. Insignificant flowers often appear on young plants.

Difficult but worth the effort

Cocos nucifera This is the coconut palm, and it is usually grown as a novelty with the large nut clearly visible at the base. Even a young plant can be 1.8m (6ft) tall, and it is difficult to keep in the home. *Cocos weddeliana* A slow-grower. Can be used in a bottle garden.

ABOVE RIGHT: Howeia belmoreana *is sometimes sold under its other name of Kentia belmoreana.*

RIGHT: Cocus nucifera *is a big palm that is quite difficult to keep in the home.*

FAR RIGHT: Chamaedorea elegans *is a palm to choose if you want one that is easy and dependable. It will remain compact enough to use on a table-top.*

Dealing with brown leaves

It is natural for the lower leaves on palms to turn brown and die in time. To keep the plant looking smart, cut these off close to the point of origin (top). Secateurs (floral scissors) are adequate for most palms, but a saw may be required for specimens with very tough leaves. If the tips of the leaves turn brown, trim them off with scissors, but avoid actually cutting into the healthy leaf (above).

Variegated plants

VARIEGATED FOLIAGE PLANTS WILL BRING COLOUR AND A TOUCH OF THE
EXOTIC INTO A DULL CORNER OR BRIGHT WINDOWSILL, DEPENDING ON THE
TYPE. UNLIKE FLOWERING PLANTS, MOST REMAIN COLOURFUL FOR TWELVE
MONTHS OF THE YEAR.

Variegation has evolved for several reasons, and the two main ones are important to understand if you want to grow healthy-looking plants with good variegation.

Many variegated houseplants are derived from forest-floor dwellers in which variegation is useful where they occur in lighter areas, such as on the edge of clearings, because it reduces the area of functional leaf. This type of variegation is frequently white and green, the white areas cutting down the area that is reactive to sunlight. This group of plants often has the best variegation when positioned away from direct light.

Others are light-demanding species and have acquired colours and patterns for other reasons. Red and pink leaves are able to absorb light from different parts of the spectrum to green leaves, for example, and many different colours in the one leaf may make it more efficient. The variegation on these plants is often better if positioned in good light.

A few plants have colourful leaves to attract pollinators. The common poinsettia (*Euphorbia pulcherrima*), and bromeliads such as neoregelia, are able to change the colour of the leaves that surround the insignificant flowers from green to bright colours such as reds and pinks.

There are other reasons for variegation, such as a being a warning to predators, so there can be no simple rules that apply to all colourful foliage plants. Some, such as coleus and crotons (codiaeums) need bright light;

others like fittonias, with their white or pale pink variegation, must be kept out of direct sun.

Potential problems

Some plants lose their strong variegation if the light is too strong, others if it is too weak. If the plant seems unhappy, move it to a lighter or shadier position as appropriate.

If any isolated, all-green shoots appear on an otherwise satisfactorily variegated plant, cut them back to the point of origin. Some plants will 're-vert' and the all-green part of the plant will eventually dominate unless you remove the offending shoots.

Coloured bracts (the modified leaves that frame a cluster of flowers) will lose their colour or intensity of colour outside the flowering period. You can do nothing about this.

Begonia rex leaves
Although they are unlikely to be labelled as specific varieties, you can collect a whole range of *Begonia rex* with different variegations. Two other types of foliage begonias are shown here: *B. masoniana* (top left) and, to the right of this, *B.* 'Tiger'.

GOING FOR A COLLECTION

There are so many variegated houseplants that some people like to start a collection of a particular group of them. This makes it easy to provide the right conditions for all of them, and the searching out of new species or varieties to add to the collection adds another dimension to the hobby.

Good plants to collect are begonias (there are many variations among *B. rex*, but lots of other begonias have interesting variegation), caladiums (if you like a challenge), codiaeums, dracaenas and cordylines, marantas and calatheas, and pileas. Named varieties of vegetatively propagated coleus are difficult to obtain, but a packet of seeds will give you an amazing range of colours and variegation from which to select those to keep.

OPPOSITE TOP: Begonia rex *varies in leaf colouring from one plant to another, but all are attractively variegated and make bold foliage plants.*

OPPOSITE LEFT: Cordyline terminalis, *also sold as* Dracaena terminalis, *comes in many varieties, the difference being in the colouring and variegation.*

OPPOSITE RIGHT: Dracaena marginata *is a popular houseplant, and there are varieties with attractively variegated leaves.*

TOP LEFT: Ficus benjamina 'Starlight' *is an outstanding houseplant with brightly variegated leaves on a plant that will eventually make a tall specimen with attractively arching shoots.*

TOP RIGHT: Ivies *(varieties of* Hedera helix*) are versatile plants that can be used as climbers or trailers.*

RIGHT: Codiaeums, *also known as crotons, can be demanding to grow well, but they make spectacular plants. Leaf hue and shape vary greatly according to variety, but all are bright and colourful.*

Graceful ferns

FERNS ARE FASCINATING PLANTS THAT WILL ADD A SPECIAL CHARM TO ANY

ROOM IN WHICH YOU WANT TO CREATE A FEELING OF COOL TRANQUILLITY

AND GREEN LUSHNESS. THEY BESTOW A RELAXED ATMOSPHERE IN CONTRAST

TO THE VIVID COLOUR OF BRIGHTER FOLIAGE PLANTS AND THE BRASHNESS OF

SOME FLOWERS.

FERN SELECTOR

Good for beginners
Asplenium nidus
Cyrtomium falcatum (syn. *Polystichum falcatum*)
Nephrolepis exaltata
Pellaea rotundifolia

For the more experienced
Adiantum capillus-veneris
Platycerium bifurcatum
Polypodium aureum
Pteris cretica (and its varieties)

Difficult but interesting
Asplenium bulbiferum
Davallia fejeenis

Ferns are grown mainly for the grace and beauty of their fronds, and their elegance compensates for their lack of flowers.

The majority of ferns will thrive in shade or partial shade, conditions that are easily provided in any home. Unfortunately they also require lots of moisture and high humidity, both of which are in short supply in the average living-room. If you want ferns to thrive, you will have to choose easy and tolerant varieties (see the *Fern Selector* above right) or provide them with the humidity and moisture that is so vital. Although most of the ferns sold as houseplants come from tropical regions and benefit from warmth, central heating spells death to many of them unless you counteract the dry air by taking measures to increase the humidity, at least immediately surrounding the plants.

The ideal place for ferns is in a conservatory, porch or garden room where it is easier to establish a moist atmosphere.

Not all ferns need coddling, however, and some have adapted to dry air or cool temperatures. There are sure to be some ferns that you can grow successfully, and if you are determined to grow the delicate types with the feathery fronds, you can try planting them in a bottle garden or terrarium where they will thrive.

Starting with ferns

If you haven't grown ferns before, start with the easy ones. As you gain experience, add some of the more exotic and difficult species.

The commonest ferns are inexpensive, and even the more unusual kinds are usually cheap if you choose small specimens.

Florists and garden centres sell the most popular houseplant ferns, but you may have to buy the less common ones from a specialist nursery.

Propagating ferns

The simplest way to increase your ferns is to divide a large clump, or remove offsets. Some, like *Davallia fejeenis*, send out rhizomes that root and can be used to grow new plants.

LEFT: *Most of the aspleniums are much easier to care for than the ferns with very thin and finely divided leaves. Asplenium nidus (left) has broad leaves that radiate from a central well or 'nest' and is a particularly good houseplant.*

:hers produce small bulbils or even
.lantlets on the leaves (*Asplenium bul-
iferum* is one). These will usually root
.to moist compost if pressed into the
.irface. These are interesting and fun
.ays to grow more ferns.

Growing your own ferns from
.oores is possible but slow, and you
.1ay find it difficult to obtain fresh
.oores of houseplant species with good
.ermination.

Don't be deceived!

Many plants commonly regarded as
ferns simply masquerade under that
name. Some, like the selaginellas, are
also primitive plants, other such as
asparagus 'ferns' are more evolved
flowering plants that simply have fine,
feathery-looking foliage – an attribute
associated with ferns. The asparagus
fern is in fact a member of the lily
family, though you would hardly

recognize the connection from its insignificant flowers.

Selaginellas are pretty, low-growing
plants that like the same conditions as
indoor ferns: damp shade and moderate warmth. They will happily grow
alongside ferns in a bottle garden.

Several asparagus ferns are available
as houseplants, all of them tougher
and more tolerant of neglect than the
majority of true ferns.

Mounting a stag's horn

.he *Platycerium bifurcatum* is a native of
.ustralia and unlike most ferns it does not
.iind a dry atmosphere. One of the most
.pectacular ways to display it is mounted on
.ark. Keep the root-ball damp and mist the
.lant regularly.

. Find a suitably sized piece of bark. Cork
.ark is ideal and you can usually buy this
.rom a florist or aquarium shop. Start with a
.mall plant and remove it from the pot. If
.ecessary, remove some of the compost to
.educe its bulk, then wrap the roots in damp
.phagnum moss. Secure the moss with wire.

.. Bind the mossy root-ball to the cork bark,
.ising florists' wire or plastic-covered wire to
.iold it securely.

ABOVE: Adiantum capillus-veneris, *like
most of the maidenhair ferns, demands a
humid atmosphere to do well. However, this
is a truly graceful species.*

ABOVE RIGHT: Cyrtomium falcatum *is the
one to choose if you find ferns generally too
demanding. This one will tolerate a much
drier atmosphere than most, and does not
need a lot of warmth.*

RIGHT: Nephrolepsis exaltata *is one of the
best ferns for a pedestal or table-top display.
There are several varieties, with variation
in leaf shape, some being more 'ruffled'
than others.*

Cacti and succulents

SOME PEOPLE ARE FASCINATED BY CACTI AND THEY BECOME A PASSIONATE

HOBBY, OTHERS DISMISS THEM AS BEING NOT QUITE 'REAL' HOUSEPLANTS.

WHATEVER YOU THINK OF THEM, CACTI AND SUCCULENTS ARE SOME OF THE

EASIEST PLANTS TO LOOK AFTER AND MAKE THE IDEAL CHOICE IF YOU OFTEN

HAVE TO LEAVE YOUR HOUSEPLANTS UNATTENDED.

Cacti can be very beautiful in flower, and a huge epiphyllum bloom can be almost breath-takingly beautiful, but you will probably decide whether or not to grow cacti depending on whether you like or dislike their overall shape and form. It has to be admitted that a few, like the epiphyllum just mentioned, can be ungainly and unattractive when out of bloom, but the vast majority are neat, compact and in the eyes of most people have a fascinating beauty of their own. There are species that creep and cascade, others which have hairy or cylindrical spiny columns, some with flat jointed pads, and others with globular or candelabra shapes.

Succulents are just as diverse: some are grown for their flowers, others for shape or foliage effect. There are hundreds of them readily available, and many more can be found in specialist nurseries.

Flowers of the desert

These need minimal water between mid-autumn and early spring, but plenty of sunshine at all times. As a rule, keep them cool in winter (about 10°C/50°F) to encourage flowering. Repot annually when young, but later only repot when really necessary as a small pot also hastens flowering.

Not all cacti will flower when young, so if you want some that flower freely on young plants, look for species of echinopsis, lobivia, mammillaria, notocactus, parodia and rebutia.

Forest cacti

The forest cacti, which have flattened leaf-like stems, are the most popular type of cacti. To keep them flowering well each year remember not to treat them like ordinary cacti, and follow these basic guidelines.

Exact treatment depends on the species, but they will require a resting period, when they are kept cool and watered only infrequently, usually mid-autumn to mid-winter or late winter to early spring, followed by a period of warmth when they are watered freely. They will also benefit from spending the summer in a shady spot outdoors.

LEFT: *Cacti often look better in small groups rather than as isolated specimens. In the group shown here, a grafted cactus (to the left of the arrangement) has been used to add additional interest.*

BELOW: *Epiphyllums have huge flowers and are among the most spectacular cacti in bloom. Unfortunately they look ugly and ungainly out of flower, so for most of the year you will want to relegate them to an inconspicuous spot.*

...ucculents

...ucculents vary enormously in their ...equirements – some, such as semper-...ivums, are tough and frost-tolerant, ...thers are tender and temperamental. ...lways look up the specific needs for ...ach plant, but as a rule they need very ...ood light and little water in winter.

...isplaying and collecting

...ew cacti and succulents make good ...ocal point plants – though a large ...piphyllum in a porch can be a real ...tunner – and they are generally best ...isplayed as groups in dish gardens ...hallow planters) or troughs. Cascad-...ng cacti, however, like the forest cacti ...lready mentioned, are almost always ...isplayed in isolation and look good ...n a pedestal while they are in bloom. ...ut if you have a conservatory, you can ...ry planting several of them in a hang-...ng basket.

Cacti are very collectable, and you ...an grow literally hundreds of them in ... modest-sized home. A frost-free ...reenhouse widens the scope consider-...bly, and you can rotate the plants ...ith those indoors, to maintain var-...ty and interest.

Handling cacti

Repotting a cactus can be a prickly job. Make it easier on your hands by folding up a strip of newspaper or brown paper (top). Wrap this around the plant, leaving enough paper at each end to form a handle (above).

CACTUS OR SUCCULENT?

Succulent simply means a plant that has adapted to dry conditions and can retain moisture with minimal loss from its leaves, which are often plump and fleshy. Cacti are also succulents, but in all except a few primitive species the leaves have become modified to spines or hairs and the stems have taken over the function of leaves – being thick, fleshy and with the ability to photosynthesize.

Although most cacti have their natural home in warm, semi-desert regions of America, some grow as epiphytes on trees in the forests of tropical America. Some of these, such as zygocactus, schlumbergera and rhipsalidopsis, have produced hybrids and varieties that are popular flowering houseplants in winter and spring.

ABOVE: Crassula ovata, *like most succulents, is undemanding and will thrive with just a modicum of care.*

FAR LEFT: Euphorbia trigona *is an easy-to-grow succulent with distinctive three- to four-sided branches.*

LEFT: Sansevieria trifasciata *'Laurentii' is an attractive variegated plant that is really tough and needs minimal attention.*

Bromeliads

BROMELIADS ARE STRANGE PLANTS. SOME HAVE LEAVES THAT FORM WATER-HOLDING VASES, OTHERS HAVE BRIGHTLY COLOURED LEAVES THAT MAKE A SUBSTITUTE FOR COLOURFUL FLOWERS, AND A FEW ACTUALLY GROW ON AIR AND NEED NO SOIL.

S ome bromeliads – aechmeas, vrieseas and guzmanias for example – are grown for their attractive flower heads as well as for their foliage. A few – billbergias, for example – have individual flowers that are both strange and beautiful. The vast majority are best considered as foliage plants. Some, such as neoregelias, form a rosette of leaves that becomes brightly coloured in the centre when the plants flower, others like cryptanthus are prettily variegated. The pineapple is the best-known bromeliad, but it is the variegated forms such as *Ananas comosus* 'Variegatus' that are generally grown as houseplants.

Air plants
A large group of tillandsias are known as air plants because they grow without soil. In nature they drape themselves over branches or even wires, or cling to rocks. One of the most attractive ways to display them is on a bromeliad tree (see opposite), but you can buy them displayed in shells, baskets, or even attached to a mirror with glue. You can also improvise with any suitable containers that you have around the house.

- Mist the plants regularly, especially from spring to autumn. This is the only way that they can receive moisture if the air itself is not sufficiently humid.
- Feed by adding a very dilute liquid fertilizer to the misting water, perhaps once a fortnight, when the plants are actively growing.

CARING FOR BROMELIADS

🐾 Bromeliads need special care. The following advice applies to most kinds, but see the separate instructions for air plant tillandsias.

🐾 Most kinds need only moderate warmth (about 10°C/50°F), but some need 24°C/75° to flower.

🐾 Give them good light, out of direct sun (a few, such as cryptanthus and pineapples, will tolerate full sun).

🐾 Grow in small pots as they don't need much compost (potting soil), and water only when the compost becomes almost dry.

🐾 Use a peat-based compost rather than one with loam, and if possible mix in perlite or sphagnum moss.

🐾 For those that form a 'vase', keep this topped up with water (rainwater in hard-water areas).

🐾 Mist the leaves in summer, and add a foliar feed occasionally. Vase types can have a one-third strength fertilizer added to the vase water every couple of weeks.

ABOVE LEFT: *Most tillandsias are popularly known as air plants because they do not need planting in compost (potting soil). They are very ornamental when mounted on a piece of bark or driftwood.*

LEFT: Neoregelia carolinae *is typical of the 'vase' bromeliads. The central leaves colour when the small flowers appear in the central vase formed by the rosette of leaves.*

OPPOSITE LEFT: Ananas bracteatus striatus *is a variegated version of the pineapple that makes a striking houseplant.*

OPPOSITE RIGHT: *Most guzmanias, like* G. lingulata, *have long-lasting flower heads.*

LOW: Aechmea fasciata
s weird but beautiful
wers, set off by bold,
yish foliage.

MAKE A BROMELIAD TREE

🦋 The size and shape of your 'tree' will depend on the space that you have available, a suitable container, and the size of your branch. Choose a forked branch from a tree and saw it to size.

Anchor the branch in the container with stones, bricks or beach pebbles – this will add weight and stability as well as holding the branch upright. Then pour in plaster of Paris or a mortar or concrete mix, to within a couple of centimetres (an inch) of the top of the container. You can set a few empty pots into the plaster or concrete to allow for planting into the base later.

When the plaster or concrete has set, wire your bromeliads to the tree. Remove most of the compost (potting soil) from the roots, and pack some sphagnum moss around them. Secure the roots to the tree with plastic-covered or copper wire. Make sure that you take advantage of any forks in the branch to hold an attractive bromeliad.

Air plant tillandsias such as *T. usneoides* can simply be draped over the branches; other species may have to be wired or glued on.

Flowering houseplants

FLOWERING HOUSEPLANTS ARE USUALLY SHORT-LIVED IN THE HOME, BUT THEY BRING A SPLASH OF COLOUR AND VIBRANCY THAT NOT EVEN COLOURED FOLIAGE CAN ACHIEVE. THEY ALSO ADD AN ELEMENT OF SEASONAL VARIATION THAT FOLIAGE PLANTS LACK.

The most rewarding flowering houseplants are those that grow bigger and better each year, with each subsequent blooming crowning another year of good cultivation and care. Flowers that you should be able to keep growing in the home from year to year include beloperones, bougainvilleas, *Campanula isophylla*, clivias, gardenias, hoyas, *Jasminum polyanthum*, *Nerium oleander*, pelargoniums, saintpaulias, spathiphyllums and streptocarpus.

The disposables

Many flowering pot plants are difficult to keep permanently in the home and are best discarded when flowering has finished (or in some cases placed in a greenhouse if you have one). They are no less valuable indoors, and should be

regarded rather like long-lasting cu flowers. A lot of them are annuals an can, therefore, be inexpensively raise from seed: try browallias, calceolarias cinerarias and exacums, which are a bright and cheerful, inexpensive t buy and not difficult to raise from see yourself.

Annuals die after flowering an have to be discarded, but others ar just not worth the effort of trying t

LEFT: Begonia elatior *hybrids can be in flower for most months of the year, but plants like the dwarf narcissus 'Tete-a-Tete are especially welcome because of their seasonal nature.*

BELOW LEFT: *Varieties of* Kalanchoe blossfeldiana *are available in flower the year round.*

BELOW: *Pot-grown lilies make striking houseplants, but it is usually better to buy them in flower rather than try to grow your own from bulbs. Commercial growers can ensure that suitable dwarf varieties are used, and chemicals are often employed to keep the plants compact. Plant them in the garden to flower in future years.*

save in home conditions: impatiens are often leggy if saved, and easy to raise or cheap to buy; Hiemalis begonias quickly deteriorate and are difficult to keep healthy, furthermore, they are so cheap to buy that it's hardly worth taking up valuable space with them once flowering is over. Garden bulbs like hyacinths may bloom beautifully if forced for early flowering, but they will fail to give an acceptable repeat performance and are therefore best put out in the garden to recover and give a garden display in future years.

Hardy border plants such as astilbes are sometimes sold as pot plants. They look magnificent in flower, but the pot of large leaves left afterwards is hardly attractive, and the plant is almost sure to deteriorate if kept indoors. By planting it in the garden after flowering you will have enjoyed plumes of beauty for a few weeks after purchase, then years of pleasure in the garden afterwards.

Tricked into flowering

Some plants are tricked into flowering at a particular time, or into blooming on compact plants. You won't be able to reproduce these conditions in the home. Year-round chrysanthemums are made to bloom every month of the

RIGHT: *Saintpaulias are among the most popular flowering plants, and there are so many variations in flower shape, size and colour that you can easily form an interesting collection of them.*

BELOW LEFT: *Hydrangeas make attractive houseplants if bought in flower, but they do not make easy long-term residents in the home. Try planting them in the garden when they have finished flowering.*

BELOW RIGHT: *Impatiens have always been popular houseplants, but the New Guinea types have bolder foliage than the older types usually grown. Some also have striking variegated leaves, as a bonus to the pretty flowers.*

year by having their day length adjusted by special lighting and by blacking out the greenhouse. They will probably be blooming on compact plants because they have been treated with dwarfing chemicals, the effects of which gradually wear off. If you manage to keep them going, they will become taller and probably flower at a different time. Try planting them in the garden – some varieties will thrive as garden plants if the winters are not too severe.

The poinsettia (*Euphorbia pulcherrima*) is another plant that is controlled by manipulating day length and in which height is also chemically controlled. Some people keep them successfully for future years, but they become taller plants, and the colourful bracts are produced at a different time of year unless their day length is controlled. This can be done by covering with a black polythene bag for fourteen hours a day for eight weeks. It is much easier to buy new plants.

Kalanchoes are also induced to flower outside their normal period by adjusting day length in the same way.

BRIGHT BERRIES

Don't overlook plants with bright berries. These will often remain attractive for much longer than flowers; some of the most popular ones are easily raised from seed and are relatively inexpensive if you have to buy them. Annual peppers (*Capsicum annuum*) have cone-shaped fruits in shades of yellow, red, and purple. *Solanum capsicastrum* has orange or red berries shaped like small tomatoes – and with luck you can keep the plant going for another year, placing it outdoors for the summer. Remember to keep the air humid by misting periodically to prevent berries dropping prematurely.

Opposite above: Year-round chrysanthemums make excellent short-term houseplants. They are best bought in bud or flower then enjoyed for a few weeks before being discarded.

Opposite below: Berries can be as bright as flowers, and often last for much longer. Those of Solanum capsicastrum *and* S. pseudocapsicum *and their hybrids look like cherry-sized tomatoes. The plants are usually discarded after flowering but can be kept for another year.*

Top left: Beloperone guttata *is easy to grow, long-lasting in flower, and you should be able to keep it from year to year.*

Top right: Primula obconica *is a delightful houseplant when it is in flower. However, some people have an allergic reaction to the leaves.*

Centre right: The azalea most commonly sold as a pot plant, and sometimes called Azalea indica, *is botanically* Rhododendron simsii.

Right: Euphorbia pulcherrima, *the so-called poinsettia, has insignificant true flowers, but really spectacular and colourful bracts to surround them.*

GARDEN ANNUALS

If you have a few spare plants after planting out the summer bedding, it might be worth potting some of them up into larger pots to use indoors. Among those that can make attractive short-term house-plants if the position is light enough are ageratums, lobelias, salvias and French marigolds.

Scent in the air

SCENT ADDS ANOTHER DIMENSION TO YOUR PLANTS, AND IT'S NOT ONLY FLOWERS THAT ARE FRAGRANT. TAKE ANOTHER JOURNEY OF DISCOVERY WITH SOME OF THE AROMATIC HOUSEPLANTS THAT WILL MAKE YOU WONDER WHY YOU EVER USED CHEMICAL AIR FRESHENERS.

ABOVE: *The flowers of* Gardenia jasminoides *are pure white in full bloom, darking to a creamy-yellow with age, and are richly fragrant.*

BELOW LEFT: Datura suaveolens *(syn.* Brugmansia suaveolens*) is a large and magnificent plant, with huge bell-like flowers and a strength of scent that matches the size of the blooms. This variety is* 'Grand Marnier'.

Perception of scent is an individual experience, and one that is more developed in some individuals than in others. Our ability to detect scents can be affected by the way in which our scent receptors are genetically determined. Some people are scent blind in the same way in which some people are colour blind. They can detect most smells but have a deficiency in certain types: someone who can smell a rose or a sweet pea might be unable to appreciate the equally potent perfume of the freesia. This makes it difficult to recommend specific plants to others without qualification: the plants suggested here have a smell readily detected by most people, but you may find a particular scent weak or even indiscernible.

Scent is further complicated by individual reactions to a scent when it is detected. Sometimes this may be for biochemical reasons, but it may even be that some scents are associated with pleasant or unpleasant experiences. There are scented-leaved geraniums (pelargoniums) that might remind one person of the tangy fragrance of lemons while another may detect a thymol smell in them that reminds them of an earlier visit to a dentist.

The only way to discover whether you like the scent of a particular plant

is to grow it and sniff it. You wil almost certainly like those suggestec below, but if you don't, simply cros them off your list for the future.

Placing scented plants

Plants that have a delicate fragrance which you have to sniff at close quarters, such as an exacum, need to be positioned where sniffing is easy – perhaps on a table or shelf that you pass in the hall, or as a centrepiece for the dining table.

Plants with a dominant scent, like gardenias and hyacinths, can be so potent that one plant will fill the whole room with scent. It doesn't matter where you place these in the room, but avoid other fragrant plants that may conflict with them; place these in another room where you can appreciate their own distinct fragrances in isolation.

ABOVE: Stephanotis floribunda *is a very fragrant climber that can be grown as a pot plant while young.*

ABOVE CENTRE: *A bowl of hyacinths will fill a room with scent. Although they are at their best for perhaps a week, by planting different varieties, and using ordinary bulbs and those specially treated for early flowering, you can enjoy them over a period of months.*

ABOVE RIGHT: *Scented-leaved geraniums (pelargoniums) usually have insignificant flowers. Grow them for their aromatic foliage and position them where you might accidentally brush against them, or can touch the leaves to release their pungent fragrance. This is* Pelargonium graveolens, *with a scent reminiscent of lemons.*

BELOW: *Oranges make superb conservatory plants, and can be brought into the house for short spells.*

FRAGRANT FOLIAGE

Some of the best plants to grow for fragrant foliage are the scented-leaved geraniums (pelargoniums). These are just of few of them:
P. *capitatum* (rose-scented)
P. *crispum* (lemon-scented)
P. *graveolens* (slightly lemony)
P. *odoratissimum* (apple-scented)
P. *tomentosum* (peppermint-scented)

Plants that you have to touch or brush against to release the scent, like scented-leaved geraniums (pelargoniums), should be placed where you might come into contact with them accidentally, or intentionally, as you pass: alcoves or windows by a flight of stairs and on the kitchen table or worktop, for example.

SCENTED FLOWERS

Citrus (fragrant flowers, citrus-scented foliage and fruit)
Datura suaveolens
Exacum affine
Hyacinths
Hymenocallis × *festalis*, H. *narcissiflora*
Jasminum officinale
Narcissus 'Paperwhite'
Stephanotis floribunda

Orchids and other exotics

ADD A TOUCH OF CLASS TO YOUR COLLECTION OF HOUSEPLANTS BY GROWING

A FEW ORCHIDS, ALONG WITH OTHER EXOTICS, SUCH AS STRELITZIA, THE

'BIRD OF PARADISE FLOWER'.

O rchids have a reputation for being difficult to grow and, consequently, many people are deterred from trying them as houseplants. If you choose the right types, however, they are relatively undemanding and should make larger and more impressive clumps each year.

The drawback to orchids is the contrast between the beauty of their exotic flowers and the rather ungainly foliage with which you have to live for the other ten or eleven months of the year. The best way to grow them is to stand the plants in a sheltered and partially shaded spot in the garden during the summer – or better still in a conservatory if you have one – and then to bring them indoors for the winter or when they are coming into flower.

Easy orchids

The best orchids to start with are cymbidium hybrids, which are easy to grow, readily available and inexpensive to buy if you are not fussy about a particular variety.

Miltonias are a better choice if you want a more compact plant. The large, flat, pansy-like flowers come in a range of brilliant colours, and will often last for a month.

Cypripediums (paphiopedilums) are another group of distinctive and easy orchids to try. Sometimes called slipper orchids, the bottom petals form a slipper-shaped pouch.

Other orchids can be grown indoors, especially if you are able to create a special area for them, perhaps with artificial light, but it is best to gain experience first with the easy genera described above.

Other exotics

Try some of the following exotic-looking flowering plants that will bring some of the brilliance and flamboyance of the tropics to your home.

Anthuriums have vivid pink, red or orange 'flowers' that will never be ignored. The 'flower' is actually a spathe and it is the curly tail-like spadix that contains the true flowers. The 'flowers' are long-lasting and the foliage is attractive too.

Bougainvilleas are at their best climbing into the roof of a conservatory, but you could try one in a porch or light window. The bright 'flowers' are actually papery bracts. Prune after flowering and keep cool but frost-free for the winter.

Grooming orchids
With age, orchid leaves often become blemished. If the damage is towards the end of the leaf, try cutting it away. Angle the cut to make the end a more natural shape than if cut at right-angles.

Daturas are big plants, really at their best in a conservatory, although you can use small plants indoors. The huge bell-like flowers are usually white, pink or yellowish, depending on the species and variety. The heady scent matches the magnificence of the blooms, and even a single flower can almost fill a small house with scent in the evening.

Hibiscus rosa-sinensis grows into quite a large shrub but can be bought as a small plant. The blooms are big and beautiful: 10cm (4in) or more across, in shades of red, yellow and almost orange.

Strelitzias are sometimes called 'bird of paradise flowers' because the orange and blue flowers are thought to resemble the head of an exotic-looking bird. The leaves are often 1m (3ft) or more tall, and a large plant is truly spectacular.

HOW TO GROW ORCHIDS

It is best to check the specific requirements for each species, but the following rules apply to most:

Place them in a very light position, but not in direct, strong sunlight.

Provide plenty of humidity. Stand the pots on a gravel tray, or mist regularly. Small plants do well in an enclosed plant case.

Avoid draughts, but provide plenty of ventilation. Move them away from a cold window at night.

Repot only when the pot is full of roots. Always use a special potting mixture recommended for orchids (you may have to buy it from a specialist nursery).

Feed regularly during the summer.

Stand the plants outdoors in a sheltered position for the summer if you don't have a conservatory to put them in.

Water only when the compost (potting soil) is almost dry.

OPPOSITE TOP: Strelitzia reginae, *the 'bird of paradise flower', never fails to impress with its flamboyant flowers.*

OPPOSITE CENTRE: *The red or pink 'petals' that surround the insignificant proper flowers of the striking anthuriums are in fact modified leaves.*

TOP: *Bougainvilleas have a really exotic look, and although they are climbers can be used as a houseplant while small. Larger plants are best in a conservatory.*

ABOVE: *Phalaenopsis orchids will flower in most months of the year, but they are not easy plants to grow in the home.*

ABOVE RIGHT: *Cymbidiums are among the easiest orchids to grow in the house, but even so they usually benefit from a spell outdoors or in the greenhouse during the summer months.*

RIGHT: Hibiscus rosa-sinensis *blooms are big, bold and bright; they seldom fail to attract attention.*

Fun plants

SOME PLANTS ARE ENTERTAINING OR EDUCATIONAL RATHER THAN BEAUTI-

FUL. THEY ARE A GOOD WAY TO INSTILL CHILDREN WITH AN APPRECIATION

OF PLANTS, BUT SOME OF THEM MAKE INTERESTING HOUSEPLANTS TOO.

Carnivorous plants always fascinate children. Few of them are beautiful, though some have quite pretty flowers. *Pinguicula grandiflora* has pretty pink flowers like violets on long stalks that seem to last for weeks. Most have uninteresting flowers, however, and their attraction lies solely in the various forms of trap.

Some cannot be grown satisfactorily in the home, but the following are worth trying: *Dionaea muscipula* (a snap trap), *Drosera capensis* (an adhesive trap), *Pinguicula grandiflora* (a 'fly paper' trap), and *Sarracenia flava* (a pitfall trap). Enthusiasts grow dozens of different kinds, but these represent four different types of trap and all make quite acceptable houseplants, though they must be treated with care if they are not to be short-lived.

Sensitive plants
Several plants are sensitive to touch, collapsing on contact. The most widely available one is *Mimosa pudica*, which makes quite a pretty plant with its sensitive leaflets and attractive flowers like pink balls. It's easy to raise from seed if you can't find plants in local nurseries or garden centres.

Leaves that bear 'babies'
Some plants have the ability to produce small plantlets on the leaves, which eventually fall and root (or you can speed things up by removing them and potting them up).

Two that are quite widely available are *Kalanchoe daigremontiana* (syn. *Bryophyllum daigremontianum*), which has miniature plants all around the edge of the leaf, and *K. tubiflora* (syn.

Bryophyllum tubiflorum), which produces them in clusters at the ends of the leaves.

Other widely available plants that produce ready-made 'babies' are the fern *Asplenium bulbiferum* and *Tolmiea menziesii* (young plantlets form at the base of mature leaves).

Bulbs that flower without soil
For a novelty, try flowering colchicums 'dry'. You can just stand them
in the windowsill after purchase, but
for stability it is best to place them on
a saucer of sand. Usually within
weeks, the large crocus-like flowers
emerge from the dry bulb.

An unusual bulb called *Sauromatum
venosum* (syn. *S. guttatum*) is sometimes
sold as a novelty for flowering 'dry'
(treat like the colchicums). The tube-
like flower that eventually emerges is
sinister greenish-purple. This
strange flower will soon make its presence known by the awful stench of
carrion – fascinating for children, but
not something to have in your living-
room for long!

OPPOSITE ABOVE: Colchicum autumnale
*can be grown 'dry'. Either stand the corms
directly on a windowsill or place them in a
saucer of sand or pebbles for stability, and
wait just a few weeks for the large crocus-
like flowers to emerge.*

OPPOSITE BELOW: Dionaea muscipula *is a
carnivorous plant with a snap trap that
quickly closes over its prey.*

TOP RIGHT: Sarracenia flava *is a
carnivorous plant with a pitfall trap.*

CENTRE RIGHT: Drosera capensis *is an
example of an adhesive trap, and makes an
interesting addition to a collection of
carnivorous plants.*

LEFT AND ABOVE: Kalanchoe
daigremontiana (*syn.* Bryophyllum
daigremontianum*) produces plantlets
along the edges of its leaves (left). These often*

*fall and root into the compost (potting soil)
around the parent plant, but you can easily
remove them to pot up for a supply of plants to
give to friends (above left).*

CARING FOR CARNIVOROUS PLANTS

❧ Don't use an ordinary potting compost. It needs to be acidic and low in soluble minerals. A suitable compost (medium) usually includes peat (peat moss), sand, sphagnum moss, and sometimes perlite or finely chipped bark.

❧ Grow a collection of them in a plant case or old aquarium. Cover it if possible, to create a humid environment.

❧ Provide good light.

❧ Stand the pots on trays of gravel filled with water to provide humidity if not in an enclosed environment.

❧ Some species prefer a constantly wet compost and you can stand these in a saucer that is kept topped up with water (not advisable for normal houseplants).

❧ Only ever use soft water (distilled or deionized would do, but rain-water is best).

❧ It is best not to use a fertilizer. Most may be harmful, and if you think the plants really do need feeding, try misting them with a foliar feed made up at quarter strength, about once a fortnight during the period of active growth.

❧ These plants catch prey to obtain nutrients, but indoors the number of insects available to them will be limited. Some people release fruit flies near them or feed them with fly maggots (often available from fishing tackle shops).

Caring for houseplants

IF YOU WANT YOUR HOUSEPLANTS TO THRIVE, THEY NEED CARING FOR AND NURTURING. YOU HAVE TO CHOOSE AND BUY WISELY, UNDERSTAND THE NEEDS OF INDIVIDUAL PLANTS AND MAKE GROOMING A REGULAR JOB, JUST LIKE WATERING AND FEEDING.

Shopping for houseplants

SHOPPING FOR NEW AND INTERESTING HOUSEPLANTS CAN BE FUN, BUT BE

WARY ABOUT WHERE AND WHEN YOU BUY. A PLANT THAT HAS BEEN POORLY

TREATED BEFORE YOU BUY IT MAY ONLY REVEAL THE ILL-TREATMENT AFTER

YOU GET IT HOME.

Choosing houseplants requires as much thought and care as the purchase of anything else for the home. Indeed, some plants will be with you for much longer than many household items.

You can buy a plant simply because you like the look of it, then try to find a suitable spot; or decide what you need to fill a particular niche in the home, before going out to buy an appropriate plant. The latter is undoubtedly the theoretical ideal, but it overlooks reality.

Except for the most common houseplants, the chances of finding a particular plant, even over several shopping trips, is not great and, more importantly, you may overlook a beautiful plant that you hadn't previously considered. Part of the fun of growing plants is to come across unexpected discoveries, plants that you've never seen before. Although advance planning is desirable, never be deterred from the impulse buy of something interesting or unusual, especially if you are prepared for a few failures along the way.

Where to buy

For everyday houseplants, a garden centre is often the best place to buy: there is likely to be a reasonable selection of 'basic' houseplants, and usually at least a few uncommon kinds. Most importantly, they will almost certainly be in conditions similar to a greenhouse: good light, warmth (ventilated in summer), with a buoyant and humid atmosphere. Staff are also

ABOVE: *Try to buy your houseplants from a nursery or garden centre where they have excellent growing conditions in good light.*

GETTING THEM HOME

🌿 Buy your plants last, immediately before you go home.

🌿 Don't put plants in a hot car boot (trunk), especially if you don't plan to drive straight home, or if the drive is a long one.

🌿 Make sure that they are wrapped in a protective sleeve if carrying them home by public transport. This will protect them from cold and wind, and guard against knocks.

usually knowledgeable, but beware assuming that part-time or tempora[ry] staff know more than you do!

Florists also sell pot plants bu[t] except for the very largest shops, t[he] range is inevitably limited and cond[i]tions are seldom good. Some floris[ts] have pavement displays outside t[he] shop, in which they include pot plan[ts] as well as cut flowers. Avoid these: y[ou] run the same risks as with mark[et] stalls (outdoor stands), where at lea[st] the price is usually cheaper.

Some large stores sell a limit[ed] range of plants. At the best of the[se] the quality is excellent, with t[he] plants well looked after and remov[ed] from sale if not bought within a ce[r]tain time. In others they can langui[sh] in poor light and with inadequa[te] care, slowly deteriorating until th[ey] reach the point of death. The quali[ty] and condition of plants sold by ordi[n]ary shops or home-improvement stor[es] vary enormously. Go through t[he] *Buyer's checklist* below carefully befo[re] buying from these sources.

Market stalls often sell plants [at] very competitive prices, and they a[re] usually sold quickly, so it is possib[le] to obtain quality plants cheaply if y[ou] don't mind the limited range. Bewa[re] of buying in cold weather – especial[ly] in winter. The chill plants receiv[e,] having come out of hot-house cond[i]tions, may not be obvious until a fe[w] days after you get them home, wh[en] the leaves start to drop. Even in t[he] summer, houseplants displayed ou[t]doors can suffer a severe check [to] growth if the weather is cold or wind[y.]

Buyer's checklist

● Check the compost (potting soil[).] If it has dried out the plants ha[ve] been neglected. Don't buy.

● Lift and check the base of the po[t.] If lots of roots are coming out [of] the bottom, the plant should ha[ve] been repotted sooner. A few sma[ll] roots through the bottom of t[he] pot is not a sign of neglect, and [is] normal where the plants have be[en] grown on capillary matting.

If buying a flowering plant, make sure that there are still plenty of buds to open, otherwise the display may be brief.

Look critically at the shape. If growth is lop-sided, or the plant is bare at the base, choose another.

Make sure the plant is labelled. A label should tell you how to care for the plant, and unlabelled plants suggest a lack of concern for plants and customers.

Avoid plants with damaged or broken leaves.

Don't be afraid to turn the leaves over. Look for signs of pests and diseases. If you find any, leave them in the shop!

If the plants are displayed in a protective sleeve, don't buy unless you can remove your potential purchase for inspection. Display sleeves can hide all kinds of horrors, such as rots and diseases, pests, and even a sparse or poorly shaped plant.

rotective sleeves
hese can be useful: they help to get the ant home with minimum damage and offer me protection from cold winds in winter. ut make sure they don't hide damaged or scased leaves. Be prepared to remove the eeve to examine a plant if they are splayed in this way.

Root check
It is natural for a few roots to grow through the bottom of the pot, especially if a capillary watering system has been used (which is normal in plant nurseries), but a mass of roots growing through the pot is probably a sign that it needs repotting.

Flowering plants
When buying a flowering plant, make sure that there are plenty of buds still to open. A plant in full flower may be more spectacular initially, but the display will be shorter.

Pests and diseases
Examine the undersides of a few leaves to make sure they are free of pests and diseases before you buy.

Pot sizes

Houseplants look better, and will grow better, if they are in a pot of an appropriate size. The plant in the picture at the top of the page is in a pot that's too large – it dominates the plant. The one shown above is in a pot that's too small; not only is it top-heavy and unstable, but the amount of compost (potting soil) in the pot is unlikely to be sufficient to sustain the plant.

Creating the right environment

IT'S IMPOSSIBLE TO RECREATE THE ATMOSPHERE OF A SOUTH AMERICAN RAINFOREST OR THE SEMI-DESERT CONDITIONS OF THE WORLD'S MORE ARID REGIONS IN OUR HOMES. YET WE EXPECT ORCHIDS AND BROMELIADS TO THRIVE ALONGSIDE CACTI AND SUCCULENTS, PLANTS FROM THE WORLD'S WARMEST REGIONS TO COEXIST WITH HARDY PLANTS SUCH AS IVIES AND AUCUBAS. CREATING THE RIGHT CONDITIONS TO SUIT SUCH A DIVERSITY OF PLANTS, WHILST KEEPING A HOME THAT'S ALSO COMFORTABLE TO LIVE IN, CALLS FOR INGENUITY AND A DASH OF COMPROMISE.

Only plants that normally grow i deserts, on steppes, high mountain and barren moors grow in areas devoi of shade. And even these may not lik the sun's rays intensified throug glass. If possible, fit shades that yo can use for the hottest part of the day Even net curtains are useful in screen ing out some of the strongest rays.

The so-called shade plants do no like any direct sun, but that does no necessarily mean that they will grow in gloom. The eye is deceptive when i comes to judging light levels. Use camera fitted with a light meter, an measure the light in different parts c the room. You might discover that th light is as poor immediately above o below a window as it is in the centre c the room. If the windows are high experiment with the light meter to se how much better the light might be i

U se the advice on labels and in books as a guide to the best conditions in which to keep your plants. In reality you may not be able to accommodate all the conditions listed as desirable, but most plants will still survive even if they do not thrive. Take recommendations for humidity seriously: a plant that requires very high humidity is likely to die soon in very dry air. Recommendations regarding light and shade are important but if you get this slightly wrong the consequence is more likely to be poor variegation, perhaps scorch marks on the leaves, or drawn and lanky plants, rather than dead ones. You can usually correct the problem by moving the plant.

Temperature is the most flexible requirement, and most plants will tolerate a wide fluctuation above or below the suggested targets.

Temperature
Treat with caution advice in books and on labels that gives a precise temperature range. Most plants will survive temperatures much lower than the ones normally recommended, and, in winter when the light is poor, a high temperature may stimulate growth that can't be supported by the light levels. Upper temperature figures are meaningless unless you have air conditioning. In summer the outside temperature often rises above those recommended for particular plants, and unless you have some way of cooling the air, the plants will have to suffer the heat along with you. They will almost certainly come to no harm if shaded from direct sun and provided that the humidity is high enough.

Once the temperature drops towards freezing, however, most houseplants are at risk. Even in a centrally heated home, temperatures can drop very low if heating is turned off at night.

Light and shade
The best position for most plants is in good light but out of direct sun. Even plants that thrive in sun outdoors may resent the strongly magnified rays through glass, which will often scorch the leaves. Be especially wary of positioning plants behind patterned glass in full sun: the pattern can magnify the sun's rays.

Effects of heat
Leaf scorch (brown marks or blotches that leave the areas looking thin and papery) is a common problem on plants placed on a very sunny windowsill. Unless they are adapted to this kind of intense heat, the tissue of the leaves can be damaged. The problem is most likely if drops of water are left on the foliage in bright sunlight (the water acts like a magnifying glass) or where patterned glass intensifies the sun's rays as it acts like a lens

ABOVE: *Plants like schizanthus and cinerarias will make a super show if you can provide good light and humid conditions.*

ou raised a plant on a pedestal or ositioned it on a low table.

Humidity

Humidity – or the amount of moisture present in the air at a given temperature – is important to all plants, but especially those with thin or delicate leaves, such as ferns, selaginellas and aladiums. Grow those plants that need a very humid atmosphere in a bottle garden or plant case, or mist the plants frequently (at least once a day, more often if possible).

For less demanding plants that still need high humidity, grow them in groups to create a microclimate or stand the plants on gravel, pebbles or marbles in a shallow dish containing water. Provided that the bottom of the pot is not in direct contact with the water the air will be humid without the compost becoming waterlogged. Misting is still desirable, but if the plants are in flower shield the blooms while you do so, otherwise the petals may become marked or begin to rot.

Simple humidity trays to place over radiators are inexpensive and help to create a more buoyant atmosphere for houseplants.

Increasing humidity
It can be difficult to create a humid environment in the home, but a small microclimate can be created around the plant. Standing the plant over a dish containing water will increase the humidity, but the pot must be stood on small pebbles or marbles to keep it above water level and avoid waterlogged compost (potting soil).

Misting foliage plants
The majority of houseplants will benefit from misting with water. If you can do it daily the plants will almost certainly grow better. Delicate ferns that need a very high humidity may need misting several times a day for really good results.

Misting flowering plants
Although the foliage benefits from misting, water can damage delicate flowers. Simply protect the blooms with a piece of paper or cardboard if the plant is in flower.

Windowsill plants

WINDOWSILLS ARE A FAVOURITE POSITION FOR HOUSEPLANTS, BUT YOU
NEED TO CHOOSE PLANTS APPROPRIATE TO THE ASPECT. NOT ALL PLANTS
APPRECIATE A BAKING IN THE SUNSHINE.

ABOVE: Hoya carnosa *is a pretty climber or*
trailer for a sunny position. It is usually
grown for its white flowers, but the
variegated 'Tricolor' also makes an
attractive foliage plant.

It is a good idea to analyse the amount of direct light coming through each window before deciding on the best spots for various plants with different light needs. Large windows obviously let in most light, but it will still be less than outdoors, and the larger the area of glass, the more rapidly temperatures drop at night.

The majority of plants flourish best when placed in good light in a position that is shaded from the direct rays of the sun. There are bound to be some rooms that receive little direct light, but most will receive some sun at least in the morning or evening. Except for shade lovers that are particularly vulnerable to direct sun, the majority of plants will benefit from this as the strength of the sun is generally weaker in the early morning and evening, so leaf scorch is less likely. The compost (potting soil) is also less likely to dry out rapidly if the sun has moved around before its midday peak.

Very sunny windows can still be packed with interest if you select the plants carefully, but be prepared to keep the compost well watered in warm weather. Avoid splashing the leaves when the sun is on them, however, as the droplets of water can act like a further magnifying glass and scorch the leaves.

The lists of suggested plants given here are not definitive, but an example of what can be grown. Be prepared to experiment with many more, especially on a light windowsill that does not receive fierce direct sun.

Where only the genus is mentioned, all the widely available species sold as houseplants should be successful.

You will find some plants listed in more than one group. Many plants will grow in sun or partial shade and a few will do well in both direct sun and indirect light.

Plants for a very sunny window

Ananas, cacti, ceropegia, chlorophytum, coleus, geraniums (pelargoniums), regal, zonal, scented-leaved, gerbera, hippeastrum, *Hoya carnosa,* hypocyrta, impatiens, iresine, *Kalanchoe blossfeldiana* and hybrids, nerium, *Plectranthus fruticosus,* sansevieria, setcreasea, stapelia, succulents (most), yucca and zebrina.

Plants for a window that receives early or late sun

Aechmea, aglaonema, anthurium, aphelandra, begonia, beloperone, billbergia, caladium, calathea, capsicum, chlorophytum, chrysanthemum, cocos, codiaeum, coleus, *Cordyline terminalis* (syn. *C. fruticosa*) and varieties, crossandra, cuphea, ficus (most), gardenia, gynura, hoya, impatiens, maranta, nertera, *Plectranthus oertendahlii,* rhipsalidopsis, saintpaulia, sansevieria, sinningia, solanum, spathiphyllum, tolmiea, tradescantia, zebrina.

Plants for a light window out of direct sunlight

Adiantum, aglaonema, anthurium, asparagus, aspidistra, asplenium, billbergia, calathea, chlorophytum, clivia, dieffenbachia, dracaena, ferns, *Ficus deltoidea, Ficus pumila,* hydrangea, maranta, orchids, saintpaulia, sansevieria, selaginella, soleirolia (syn. helxine), spathiphyllum.

ABOVE: Aphelandra squarrosa *needs good*
light but not direct summer sun. Grow it
where it just receives early or late sun in the
summer and in the best light possible in
winter.

ABOVE: *Gerberas will tolerate a very sunny*
position, but if you plan to discard the plant
after flowering you can use it to brighten up
dull spots too.

ABOVE: Mammillaria elongata, *like most cacti, will thrive in a hot, sunny position.*

ABOVE: Calathea zebrina *is best in a light position that receives early or late sun, but not direct midday sun.*

ABOVE: Aglaonema *'Silver Queen' grows well in semi-shade or bright light, but avoid direct midday sun.*

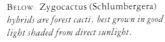

ABOVE: Yucca elephantipes *benefits from as much light as possible. It will enjoy a hot, sunny position.*

BELOW: Zygocactus (Schlumbergera) *hybrids are forest cacti, best grown in good light shaded from direct sunlight.*

ABOVE: Aechmea fasciata *is grown mainly for its fascinating flower spike. Because it grows naturally in trees, it is not adapted to life on a very hot, sunny windowsill. Position it where it receives early or late sun.*

ABOVE: Sansevieria trifasciata *'Laurentii' is one of those tough plants that will do well on any windowsill, in shade or full sun.*

RIGHT: Kalanchoe blossfeldiana *hybrids do well on a sunny windowsill.*

Shady spots

PLANTS THAT TOLERATE SHADE ARE PARTICULARLY USEFUL, ESPECIALLY IF
YOU NEED FOCAL POINT PLANTS FOR DIFFICULT POSITIONS WITHIN THE
ROOM. LARGE SPECIMEN PLANTS ARE USUALLY TOO LARGE FOR A WINDOW-
SILL SO THESE HAVE TO COMBINE SIZE WITH SHADE TOLERANCE.

It is a mistake to position a plant
purely for decorative effect, and you
should always choose a spot that the
plant will at least tolerate even if it
doesn't thrive. For really inhospitable
corners where it's just too dark even
for shade lovers, use disposable flowering plants, or even ferns if you are
prepared to discard them after a couple
of months.

In winter, plants are unlikely to
tolerate a light intensity less than
1,000 lux, and 5,000 lux in summer
is about the minimum for foliage
plants such as aspidistras and *Cissus
rhombifolia* (syn. *Rhoicissus rhomboidea*).
These are meaningless figures unless
you have a way of measuring light,
but fortunately there is a simple
rough-and-ready way that can be
used. Two methods of judging light
levels are described in *How to Assess
Light* (opposite).

ABOVE: Aglaonema *'Silver Queen' is
undemanding and useful for low-light
areas.*

ARTIFICIAL LIGHT

Artificial light can be used to
highlight plants in dull spots, and
can also be used to help plants thrive
where natural light is inadequate.

Even ordinary light bulbs can help
plants to grow by providing localized
warmth and a degree of increased
illumination. However, fluorescent
tubes are better for plant growth
and, because they generate less heat,
they can be used closer to the plant.
Light sources need to be close, and if
possible the tubes should be specially
balanced for plant growth (you can
buy these at some gardening shops
and also at aquarium suppliers).
Otherwise use the tubes in pairs with
one 'daylight' and one 'cool white'
used together.

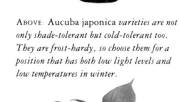

ABOVE: Aucuba japonica *varieties are not
only shade-tolerant but cold-tolerant too.
They are frost-hardy, so choose them for a
position that has both low light levels and
low temperatures in winter.*

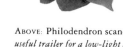

ABOVE: Ficus pumila *is a low-growing
trailer that would soon die on a sunny
window. The variegated varieties are more
attractive than the all-green species.*

ABOVE: Fatsia japonica *is a garden shrub
hardy enough to grow outside except in very
cold regions, but indoors the variegated form
is more attractive. Choose it for a low light
area where temperatures also drop in the
winter.*

ABOVE: Philodendron scandens *is a
useful trailer for a low-light area.*

ABOVE: Helsine soleirolii, *also sold as olierolia soleirolii, is a tough carpeter at will tolerate low light and cool mperatures (it will even stand some frost). here are green, silver and golden forms.*

ABOVE: *Ivies (varieties of* Hedera helix) *row happily in the wild in sun or shade, nd they will do the same in the home. If ossible provide bright conditions in winter nd avoid direct sunlight in summer.*

ABOVE: Fittonia verschaffeltii *is one of the nore difficult foliage plants to try. It will e short-lived in direct sunlight.*

ABOVE: Pellaea rotundifolia *does not 'emand such a humid atmosphere as most rns; a light window out of direct sunlight ideal.*

ABOVE: Adiantum capillus-veneris *will not tolerate a hot, sunny position for long. It will be much happier in a humid and shaded conservatory.*

ABOVE: Scindapsus aureus, *also sold as* Epipremnum aureum, *is a trailer or climber that will do well in low-light areas. This golden form is particularly bright, but in time the leaves become more green and less colourful.*

ABOVE: Asplenium nidus *is one of the easiest ferns to grow.*

HOW TO ASSESS THE LIGHT

🔋 Use a camera with a built-in light meter, and set it to a 100 ISO (ASA) film speed and 1/125 second shutter speed. Take the reading at about midday on a bright day in late spring or early summer. Position the camera where you want to place the plant, and point it towards the window.

Read off the aperture setting then use the following as a rough guide to the light level:

f16 or more = Strong light, suitable for those plants that need the best light.

f8–11 = Equivalent to screened daylight, and suitable for those plants that like good light but not strong direct sunlight.

f4–5.6 = Poor light, only suitable for those plants adapted to shade.

f2.8 = Suitable for only the most shade-tolerant species, and plants may not survive in the winter months.

🔋 Another test is to try reading a newspaper where you plan to position the plant. Assuming that you have good eyesight, the position is too dark for plants if you can't read the newspaper comfortably.

🔋 **Plants for poor light**
Aglaonema, araucaria, asplenium, aspidistra, aucuba, bulbs (such as hyacinths), but keep in good light until flowering starts, *Cissus rhombifolia* (syn. *Rhoicissus rhomboidea*) × Fatshedera, fatsia, ferns (most), *Ficus pumila*, fittonia, *Hedera helix* (ivy), palms (most), *Philodendron scandens*, pteris, sansevieria, *Scindapsus aureus* (syn. *Epipremnum aureum, Rhaphidophora aurea*), but be prepared for it to lose most of its variegation, *Soleirolia soleirolii* (syn. *Helxine soleirolii*).

Watering

NO PLANT CAN SURVIVE WITHOUT WATER, YET MORE PLANTS PROBABLY DIE FROM OVERWATERING THAN FROM UNDERWATERING. GETTING TO GRIPS WITH THIS APPARENTLY SIMPLE PROCEDURE IS ONE OF THE ESSENTIALS OF GOOD PLANT CARE.

Meters and indicator strips that are pushed into the compost help to put some kind of measurement to the amount of moisture available in the compost, but are impractical if you have a lot of houseplants. You will soon tire of pushing a probe into each pot or reading indicators left in each one. These devices are best used by beginners still gaining experience of how to judge the moisture content by other means.

How much water?
There are no fixed rules about watering. How much a plant needs, and how often, depends not only on the plant but also the kind of pot (clay pots need watering more often than plastic ones), the compost (potting soil), (peat-based composts retain more water than loam-based), and the temperature and humidity.

Watering is an acquired skill, and one that needs to be practised on an almost daily basis, otherwise it is best to switch to self-watering containers or hydroponically grown plants.

Useful techniques
Examine the pots daily if possible, using whichever of the following techniques you find the most convenient:

- Appearance alone can be a guide. Dry, loam-based composts (potting soils) look paler than when they are moist. A dry surface does not mean that the compost is dry lower down, but if it looks damp you know that you don't need to

water. If the plant is placed in a saucer, see if there is any standing water. Apart from bog plants, never add more water if there is any trace still left in the saucer.
- The touch test is useful for a peat-based compost. Press a finger gently into the surface – you will know immediately if it feels very dry or very wet.
- The bell test is useful for clay pots, especially large ones containing specimen plants and that hold a large volume of compost. Push a cotton reel onto a short garden cane

Watering from above
A small watering-can is still the most popular way to water houseplants. Choose one that is well-balanced to hold and with a long, narrow spout that makes it easy to direct the water to the compost (potting soil) rather than over the plant.

Compost (potting soil) check
If you use a clay pot, it will ring with a hollow sound if you tap it with a cotton reel on a cane or pencil and the compost is dry. If the compost is still moist the sound will be duller. With a little experience you will be able to detect the difference.

and tap the pot: a dull thud indicates moist compost (although it could also indicate a cracked pot!); a clear ring suggests dry compost. This doesn't work well with peat based composts, and not at all with plastic pots.
- With practice you can tell when the compost is dry simply by lifting the pot slightly: a pot with dry compost will feel much lighter than one with moist compost.

How to water

When you water, fill the pot to the rim – dribbles are not sufficient. If the root-ball has completely dried out, water may run straight through, down the inside of the pot, in which case stand the pot in a bucket of water until the air bubbles stop rising.

After watering, always check whether surplus water is sitting in the saucer or cache-pot. This will not matter if there are pebbles or marbles to keep the bottom of the pot out of contact with the moisture, but otherwise you must tip out the extra water. *Failure to tip out standing water is the most common cause of failure.* With just a few exceptions, if you leave most ordinary houseplants standing in water for long, they will probably die.

A long-necked watering-can is the most convenient way to water the majority of houseplants. The long neck makes it easy to reach among the leaves, and a narrow spout makes it easier to control the flow, which is also less forceful and unlikely to wash the compost (potting soil) away.

Watering with a can means that you may wet the leaves and crown of ground-hugging plants such as saint-paulias, and unless you are careful this can encourage rotting. For plants like this you may prefer to stand them in a bowl with a few centimetres (inches) of water in the bottom. Remove and allow to drain as soon as the surface of the compost becomes moist. You will probably find it less trouble, however, to be careful with a long-necked watering-can, getting the spout beneath the leaves.

Special needs

Tap water is far from ideal, but the vast majority of houseplants will tolerate it. If the water is hard (has a high calcium or magnesium content), however, you need to make special arrangements for plants that react badly to alkaline soil or compost. These include aphelandras, azaleas, hydrangeas, orchids, rhododendrons and saintpaulias. Rain-water is usually recommended for these plants, but a good supply is not always available throughout the year, and in some areas it can be polluted.

If your tap water is only slightly hard, simply filling the watering cans the day before and allowing the water to stand overnight may be sufficient. For harder water, try boiling it: part of the hardness will be deposited in the form of scale, and you can use the water once it has cooled.

Many water softeners work on a principle that unfortunately does not help the plants: if you want to benefit the plants, a demineralization system is necessary, which removes all the minerals and leaves distilled water. However, it is only worth the expense if you have a lot of plants.

Underwatering

If a plant wilts or collapses like this (top) it can usually be revived by standing the pot in a bowl of water for a few hours, then leaving it in a cool, shady position for a day. By the next day it will probably be as perky as before (above). Always make sure that the compost (potting soil) is dry before doing this, as an overwatered plant will also wilt.

Watering the outer pot
Just a few plants tolerate standing with their pots in water, like this cyperus. With these you can add water to the saucer or outer container, but never do this unless you know the plant grows naturally in marshy places.

Self-watering pots
If you find watering a chore, self-watering pots may be the answer. The moisture is drawn up into the compost (potting soil) through wicks from a reservoir below, and you will need to water much less frequently.

Overwatering
Before an overwatered plant reaches the stage of collapsing, it will probably begin to look sickly. The plant on the left has been overwatered, the one on the right has received the correct amount of water.

Feeding

FEEDING CAN MAKE THE DIFFERENCE BETWEEN A PLANT THAT SIMPLY EXISTS
AND SEEMS TO 'STAND STILL', AND ONE THAT LOOKS HEALTHY AND VIGOROUS
AND REALLY FLOURISHES. MODERN FERTILIZERS HAVE MADE FEEDING REALLY
EASY, AND NOW IT ISN'T EVEN A CHORE THAT YOU HAVE TO REMEMBER ON A
REGULAR BASIS.

Houseplants are handicapped simply by being contained in a pot. The volume of soil or compost that the roots can explore is strictly limited, and sometimes we expect the same compost to support a large plant for many years.

With a few exceptions, your plants will look better if you feed them. You can buy special fertilizers for flowering plants, foliage plants and even special groups such as saintpaulias, but if you want to keep things simple and use one type of feed for all your plants they will still respond better than if they hadn't been fed at all.

When to feed

If in doubt about a particular plant, check the label or look it up in a book. As a general rule, however, plants should be fed only when they are growing actively and when light and temperature are such that they can actually take advantage of the additional nutrients. This generally means between mid-spring and mid-autumn, but there are exceptions – notably with winter-flowering plants.

Cyclamen are fed during the winter as well as before, and the winter- and spring-flowering forest cacti are fed during the winter but rested in summer. The rule of 'active growth' is more important than the time of year.

Controlled-release fertilizers (see top right) are useful for houseplants, but bear in mind that they are influenced by temperature, so they won't stop releasing nutrients in winter as they would outdoors.

How often to apply

Some trial and error is inevitable. Books and plant labels often give advice like 'feed once a fortnight' or 'feed weekly', but with so many different formulations available such advice may be inappropriate. It assumes a typical liquid houseplant feed. Do not follow this advice too closely if you use one of the other types.

Controlled- and slow-release fertilizers

These are widely used commercially especially for outdoor container-grown plants, and also for pot plants to keep them healthy until sale. Unlike ordinary fertilizers, the nutrients are released slowly over a period of months so a couple of applications in a year is all that most plants require.

Controlled-release fertilizers are most useful for outdoor plants because they release the nutrients only when the soil temperature is high enough for the plants to make use of them.

Slow-release fertilizers are most useful for houseplants as a compost (potting soil) additive when potting up an established plant.

Why feed?
These two *Rhoicissus rhomboidea* are the same age and were the same size when bought. The plant on the left has been fed regularly and repotted once; the one on the right has not been fed and shows typical signs of starvation.

Fertilizer sticks and pellets

low-release fertilizers

low-release fertilizers are worth adding to
e compost (potting soil) because they
ustain the plants over a period of perhaps
x months. The nutrients in many peat-based
eat-moss based) or peat-substitute
omposts may become depleted within
eeks or perhaps a couple of months.

iquid feeds

iquid fertilizers are quick-acting, and
seful when a plant needs an immedi-
e boost. Strengths and dilutions
ary, so *always follow the manufacturer's
dvice* for rate and frequency of ap-
lication. Some are weak and designed
o be used at almost every watering,
thers are very strong and should be
pplied less frequently.

ellets and sticks

here are various products designed to
ake the chore out of regular feeding.
hese will save you a lot of time and
rouble in comparison with liquid
eeds, although they may work out
nore expensive in the long run. Some

Pot-plant fertilizers are also available in sticks
(top) and pellets (above) that you push into
the compost (potting soil). Many people find
these more convenient to use than having to
mix and apply liquid feeds.

are tablet-shaped, others stick-shaped,
but the principle is always the same:
you make a hole in the compost (potting soil), push in the fertilizer stick
or pellet, then leave it to release its
nutrients slowly over a period of a
month or so (check the instructions).

Slow-release sachets

Slow-release fertilizers are available in
sachets that you place inside the pot at
the bottom. These are most appropriate when repotting.

Soluble powders

These work on the same principle as
liquid feeds, but you simply dissolve
the powder in water at the appropriate
rate. They often work out less expensive than ordinary liquid fertilizers.

Granular fertilizer

If you have to add a granular or powder
fertilizer to the compost (potting soil), use a
fork to stir it into the surface, then water it in
thoroughly.

Benefits of feeding

To appreciate the benefits of feeding try
starting with two plants of the same age and
size, then feed just one of the plants
regularly. The two *Pilea cadierei* (top) are the
plants as bought. The same plants (above)
show the effect a couple of months later after
the one on the right was given just one dose
of slow-release fertilizer.

DON'T OVER-FEED

Because some feeding is good
does not mean that more feeding is
better. Do not apply more than the
manufacturer recommends,
otherwise you might kill your
plants. Salts build up in the compost
(potting soil) and can affect the
intake of water and nutrients which,
coupled with an over-stimulation of
the plant, can end in collapse.

Choosing a compost (potting soil)

YOUR PLANTS WILL ONLY BE AS GOOD AS THE COMPOST THEY GROW IN. FEEDING WILL HELP TO OVERCOME NUTRITIONAL DEFICIENCIES, BUT THE STRUCTURE OF THE COMPOST IS ALSO IMPORTANT IF THE ROOTS ARE TO GET THE RIGHT BALANCE BETWEEN MOISTURE AND AIR, SO VITAL FOR HEALTHY GROWTH. COMMERCIALLY, COMPOSTS ARE CHOSEN THAT MAKE CAPILLARY WATERING EASY, AND THAT ARE LIGHT TO TRANSPORT, BUT IN THE HOME THEY MAY NOT BE THE MOST APPROPRIATE GROWING MEDIUM.

Compost (potting soil) does more than simply anchor the plant, it acts as a reservoir for nutrients and if the structure is right achieves the right balance between moisture and air. It also acts as a host to many beneficial micro-organisms.

Earlier generations of gardeners used to formulate special potting mixtures for different types of plant, but nowadays composts are available that suit the majority of plants, and only a few have special requirements.

The main choice is between loam-based composts and those based on peat (peat moss) or a peat substitute. Most plants will grow well in either type, but there are pros and cons that may make one more or less appropriate for a particular plant.

Loam-based composts use sterilized loam as the main ingredient, with added sand and peat to improve the structure, and fertilizers to supplement the nutrients already present in the loam.

Loam composts have weight, a useful attribute for a large plant with a lot of top growth, such as a big palm, as it provides stability to the pot.

Peat-based composts are light and pleasant to handle, and many plants thrive in them. Sand or other materials are sometimes added, but all of them depend on the addition of fertilizers to support plant growth. Often the fertilizers present in the compost run out quickly, and the plants will almost certainly suffer unless you begin supplementary feeding as soon as the plants show signs of poor growth.

Peat composts are very easy to manage on a commercial scale, with automatic watering systems, but in the home they demand more careful watering than loam composts. They can dry out more completely and become difficult to re-wet, and they are also more easily overwatered.

Some gardeners are reluctant to use peat-based composts on the grounds of depleting wetland areas where peat is excavated. For that reason many alternative products are now being introduced, including composts based on coir (waste from coconuts) and finely pulverized bark. Some use a mixture of materials. Results from these alternative composts can be very variable, depending on the make and formulation. Try a number of plants in several different makes — potting up the same types of plants in each — then decide which is best.

SPECIAL MEDIUMS

🦥 A few plants have particular needs that make a general-purpose compost (potting soil) inappropriate. Lime-hating plants, such as azaleas, many begonias, ericas and saintpaulias, are the most common group, and they will grow poorly in ordinary composts. Even peat-based (peat-moss) composts are generally alkaline, because they have lime added to make them suitable for the majority of houseplants. For lime-hating plants you need an 'ericaceous' compost widely available at garden centres.

Bromeliads, cacti and orchids are other groups that have special needs, and you can buy specially formulated composts suitable for these from many specialist nurseries and good garden centres.

Perlite

Gravel

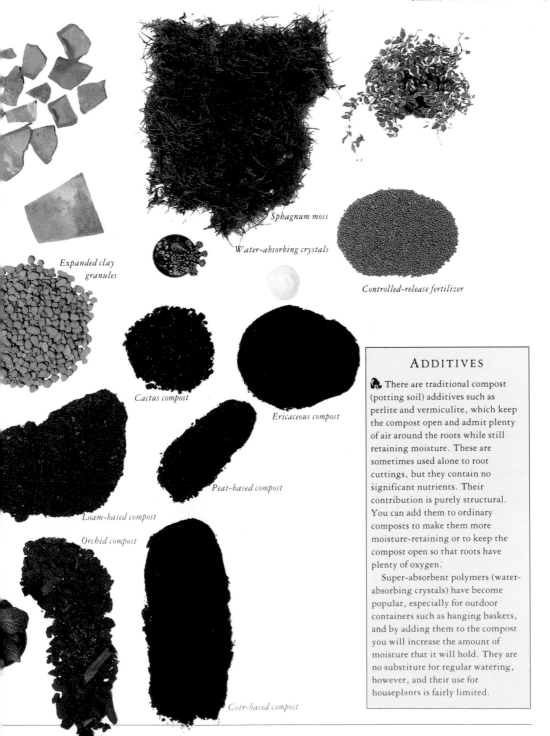

Sphagnum moss

Water-absorbing crystals

Expanded clay granules

Controlled-release fertilizer

Cactus compost

Ericaceous compost

Peat-based compost

Loam-based compost

Orchid compost

Coir-based compost

ADDITIVES

There are traditional compost (potting soil) additives such as perlite and vermiculite, which keep the compost open and admit plenty of air around the roots while still retaining moisture. These are sometimes used alone to root cuttings, but they contain no significant nutrients. Their contribution is purely structural. You can add them to ordinary composts to make them more moisture-retaining or to keep the compost open so that roots have plenty of oxygen.

Super-absorbent polymers (water-absorbing crystals) have become popular, especially for outdoor containers such as hanging baskets, and by adding them to the compost you will increase the amount of moisture that it will hold. They are no substitute for regular watering, however, and their use for houseplants is fairly limited.

Pots and containers

POTS NEEDN'T JUST BE PRACTICAL, THEY CAN BE PRETTY OR INTERESTING TOO. BUT WHATEVER TYPE YOU CHOOSE, THEIR SIZE AND PROPORTION IN RELATION TO THE PLANTS CONTAINED WILL AFFECT HOW THEY ARE PERCEIVED, AND THE POT CAN MAKE OR MAR A PLANT.

ABOVE: *This zinc container creates just the right atmosphere for an old-fashioned kitchen setting. If a container is large enough, try using a couple of compatible plants, like the adiantum and pellaea ferns used here.*

Ordinary clay or plastic pots lack visual appeal, and most people hide them in a more decorative cache-pot that is slightly larger. If you do this, put gravel, expanded clay granules or a few pebbles in the base to keep the bottom of the pot from contact with the surplus water that collects in the base. Alternatively, pack the space between the inner and outer pots with peat (peat-moss) to absorb most of the moisture, at the same time helping to create a more humid microclimate around the plant. Only use the latter method if you are very methodical about watering and are unlikely to overwater or leave stagnant water sitting at the base of the container. It will be difficult to detect and tip out once the space between the two pots has been filled.

Some plants do look good in clay pots, especially cacti and some succulents. But half-pots are often more appropriate as cacti do not have a large root system, and a shallower pot will usually look more in proportion to the plant. Half-pots have the same diameter as a full pot, but stand only about half the height. Seed pans, which are uncommon now, are similar but shallower; although intended for seed-sowing they can also be used for low or prostrate plants.

Many other plants look better in a half-pot, including azaleas, most begonias, saintpaulias and the majority of bromeliads. Be guided by the type of pot the plant is in when you buy it: if it's a shallow one, use another half-pot when you need to repot.

Some of the better quality plastic pots are coloured and come with a matching saucer, and these can look as attractive as a cache-pot, especially if you choose a colour that is co-ordinated with the room.

You can decorate ordinary clay or plastic pots by painting them freehand or using a stencil. For clay pots use masonry paint (the colours are limited, but you can compensate with a strong design), for plastic pots use acrylic artists' paints.

Square pots are more often used in the greenhouse than indoors, but they are space-saving if you have a collection of small plants such as cacti.

ABOVE: *Rush baskets can be very effective for small spring bulbs or compact plants like saintpaulias. Always line them or use them simply as a cache-pot.*

PLASTIC OR CLAY?

The vast majority of the plants on sale are grown in plastic pots: evidence that commercial growers find them satisfactory. Plastic pots are clean, light, easy to handle, remain largely free of algae and are inexpensive. They retain moisture better and the compost (potting soil) is less likely to dry out.

Perhaps surprisingly, clay pots will usually last longer than plastic ones. Plastic pots become brittle with age and even a slight knock is sometimes sufficient to break them. A clay pot won't break unless you actually drop it onto a hard surface. The extra weight of a clay pot will also be of benefit if a plant is large and rather top-heavy.

ABOVE: *Ceramic pots look stylish, and so much more colourful than an ordinary clay or plastic pot.*

ABOVE: *Bark baskets look good for houseplants that you would normally associate with trees, such as an ivy.*

ABOVE: *In a modern setting you may want a stylish type of container, like this small zinc one. The purple gynura does not detract from the container, which is a feature in its own right.*

ABOVE: *Terracotta hanging pots look more attractive than the plastic versions for a semi-cascading plant like this nephrolepis fern.*

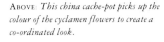

ABOVE: *This china cache-pot picks up the colour of the cyclamen flowers to create a co-ordinated look.*

ABOVE: *Moss baskets make a nice setting for a few spring plants like primroses, and crocuses. Do not plant directly into this type of container unless you can ensure the surface is protected from drips.*

ABOVE: *Keep an eye open for the unlikely or unexpected. This distinctive container is made from dried fungi! The plant in it is a variegated Ficus pumila.*

ABOVE: *Terracotta wall planters can be used indoors as well as out. This Philodendron scandens will have to be trimmed after a few months to retain the container as a feature.*

ABOVE: *This metal planter is the kind of container that would look stunning in the right setting. You can line it with moss, rather like a hanging basket.*

ABOVE: *Stoneware pots are appropriate for plants in a kitchen. This one has been planted with Helxine soleirolii (syn. Soleirolia soleirolii), which reflects the rounded shape of the pot.*

ABOVE: *Matching drip trays are useful, and this one is particularly attractive because it takes three ceramic pots.*

ABOVE: *All kinds of decorative cache-pots are available in stores and garden centres, so it should be easy to choose those that appeal to your own tastes.*

ABOVE: *Sometimes old hand-made clay pots can be used effectively. The white deposit that often appears on old pots adds to the impression of age. These have been planted with ivies.*

Potting plants

SOONER OR LATER MOST PLANTS NEED REPOTTING, AND IT CAN GIVE AN AILING PLANT A NEW LEASE OF LIFE. BUT NOT ALL PLANTS RESPOND WELL TO FREQUENT REPOTTING, AND SOME PREFER TO BE IN SMALL POTS. KNOWING WHEN TO REPOT, AND INTO WHICH SIZED POT, IS A SKILL THAT DEVELOPS WITH EXPERIENCE.

Never be in too much of a hurry to pot on a plant into a larger container. Plants do not appreciate having their roots disturbed, and any damage to them will result in some check to growth.

Repotting should never simply be an annual routine. It's a job to be thought about annually, but not actually done unless the plant needs it.

Young plants require potting on much more frequently than older ones. Once a large specimen is in a big pot it may be better to keep it growing by repotting into another pot of the same size, by topdressing, or simply by additional feeding.

When repotting is necessary

The sight of roots growing through the base of the pot is not in it itself a sign that repotting is necessary. If the plants have been watered through a capillary mat, or the pot has been placed in a cache-pot, some roots will inevitably grow through the base to seek the water.

If in doubt, knock the plant out of its pot. To remove the root-ball easily, invert the pot and knock the rim on a hard surface while supporting the plant and compost (potting soil) with your hand. It is normal for a few roots to run around the inside of the pot, but if there is also a solid mass of roots it's time to pot on.

There are several ways to repot a plant, but the two described here are among the best.

When to repot

A mass of thick roots growing through the bottom of the pot (top) is an indication that it's time to move the plant into a large one. Equally, a mass of roots curled around the edge of the pot (above) is another sign that it's time for a larger container.

Pot-in-pot method

1. Prepare the new pot as described in the *Traditional method*, if using a clay pot. However, don't cover the drainage hole at all if using a plastic pot and you intend using a capillary watering mat.

POTTING ON, POTTING UP, REPOTTING

❧ Although some of these terms are commonly used interchangeably, their true meanings are specific:

❧ **Potting up** is what happens the first time a seedling or cutting is given its own pot.

❧ **Potting on** is the action of replanting the root-ball in a larger pot.

❧ **Repotting** is sometimes taken to mean replacing the plant in a pot of the same size, but with most of the compost replaced. This is only necessary if the plant cannot be moved into a larger pot.

Place a little dampened compost (potting
l) over the base material then insert the
sting pot (or an empty one the same size),
suring that the level of the soil surface will
about 1cm (½in) below the top of the new
t when filled.

3. Pack more compost firmly between the
inner and outer pots, pressing it down gently
with your fingers. This creates a mould when
the inner pot is removed.

4. Remove the inner pot, then take the plant
from its original container and drop it into the
hole formed in the centre of the new
compost. Gently firm the compost around the
root-ball, and water thoroughly.

aditional method

Prepare a pot that is one or two sizes
ger than the original and, if the pot is a
y one, cover the drainage hole with a
ce of broken pot or a few pieces of
pped bark.

2. Make sure that the plant has been
watered a short time beforehand, and knock
the root-ball out of the old pot. Sometimes
you can remove it by pulling gently on the
plant, otherwise invert the pot and tap the
rim on a hard surface.

3. Place a small amount of compost (potting
soil) in the base of the new pot, then position
the root-ball so that it is at the right height. If
too low or too high, adjust the amount of
compost in the base.

Trickle more compost around the sides,
ning the pot as you work. It's a good idea
use the same kind of compost – peat-
at-moss) or loam-based – as used in the
ginal pot.

5. Gently firm the compost with the fingers.
Make sure there is a gap of about 1–2.5cm
(½–1in) between the top of the compost and
the rim of the pot, to allow space for
watering. Water thoroughly.

TOPDRESSING

Once plants are in large pots,
perhaps 25–30cm (10–12in) in
diameter, continual potting on into a
larger pot may not be practical. Try
removing the top few centimetres
(inches) of compost (potting soil),
loosening it first with a small hand
fork. Replace this with fresh potting
compost of the same type. This, plus
regular feeding, will enable most
plants to be grown in the same pot
for many years.

Pruning and grooming

GROOMING YOUR PLANTS OCCASIONALLY NOT ONLY KEEPS THEM LOOKING

GOOD, IT ALSO ENABLES YOU TO CHECK THEM FOR EARLY SIGNS OF PESTS AND

DISEASES BEFORE THESE BECOME A PROBLEM.

Some pruning and grooming tasks simply keep the plants looking fresh and tidy, others actually improve them by encouraging bushier growth or promoting further flowering.

Apart from picking off dead flowers, which is best done whenever you notice them, grooming is only a once-a-week task. Most jobs need doing less frequently than this, but by making a routine of tidying up your plants you will almost certainly detect pest, disease and nutritional problems that much earlier. One also learns to appreciate the plants more by close examination, so you will benefit as well as the plants.

Deadheading

This keeps the plant looking tidy, and in many cases encourages the production of more flowers. It also discourages diseases: fungus infections often start on dead or dying flowers, before spreading to the leaves.

Plants with masses of small flowers, such as fibrous-rooted begonias (*B. semperflorens*) are difficult to deadhead often enough, but unless you make some effort the flowers that fall often make a mess of the furniture or sill that they fall on, as well as spoiling the appearance of the plant itself.

Apart from where the flowers appear in a spike, remove the flower stalks as well as the flowers. Sometimes the stalks are most easily removed by hand, using a pulling and twisting motion at the same time.

If the flowers appear in spikes or large heads, such as a hydrangea, cut the whole head or spike back to just above a pair of leaves when the last blooms have finished.

Leaves

Dust and dirt accumulate on leaves as well as on furniture, but this is not always obvious unless the foliage is naturally glossy. This accumulation not only implies neglect, it [a]so harms the plant slightly by cutt[ing] down on the amount of light fall[ing] on the leaf and thereby hinder[ing] photosynthesis, the process by wh[ich] the plant produces energy for grow[th].

Wipe smooth leaves with a s[oft] damp cloth. Some people add a li[ttle] milk to the water to produce a sh[ine] on glossy foliage. The alternative i[s to] use a commercial leaf shine. Some cleaners come as aerosols or spra[ys,] others as impregnated wipes. If [you] are using an aerosol, follow the ma[nu]facturer's instructions carefully [and] pay particular attention to the rec[om]mended spraying distance.

Cloths and sprays are no use [for] cleaning hairy leaves. Instead, us[e a] small paintbrush as a duster. You [can] dust cacti in the same way.

Removing leaves
Sooner or later all plants have a few dead leaves. Even evergreens drop old leaves fr[om] time to time. Don't let them spoil the appearance of the plant; most are easily removed with a gentle tug, but tough ones may have to be cut off.

af wipes
u might find commercial leaf wipes more
nvenient to use. They leave large, glossy
ves looking shiny and bright.

Compact non-flowering plants that
n't have hairy leaves — aglaonemas
r example — can be cleaned by
rishing the foliage in a bowl of tepid
ater. But make sure that the plant
ies off out of direct sunlight, other-
se the leaves may be scorched.

aping and training
ou can improve the shape of many
useplants by pinching out the grow-
g tips to prevent them from becom-
g tall and leggy. Removing the tips
the shoots makes the plant bushier.
patiens, hypoestes, pileas and
descantias are among the many
nts that benefit from this treat-
ent. Start when the plants are
ung, and repeat it whenever the
owth looks too thin and long. This
especially useful for trailers such as
descantias: a dense, bushy cascade
out 30cm (1ft) long will look much
tter than thin, weedy-looking
oots of twice the length.
If any all-green shoots develop on a
riegated plant, pinch or prune them
ck to the point of origin.
Climbers and trailers need regular
ention. Tie in any new shoots to the
pport, and cut off any long shoots
at spoil the shape.

Deadheading
Removing dead flowers will keep the plant
looking smart, and reduce the chance of
dead petals encouraging the growth of
moulds and other diseases. Some plants also
make a mess of the table or windowsill if the
flowers are simply allowed to drop.

Sponging
Glossy-leaved plants like this ficus will look
smarter if you wipe over the foliage with
slightly soapy water occasionally. The plants
also benefit because dust can reduce the
amount of light received and also clog some
of the pores through which the plant
'breathes'.

Immersing foliage
If the plant is small enough to handle
conveniently, try swishing the foliage in a
bowl of tepid water. Do not do this if the
plant has hairy or delicate leaves.

Brushing leaves
Plants with hairy leaves, like this saintpaulia,
should not be sponged or cleaned with a leaf
wipe. Instead, brush them occasionally with a
soft paintbrush.

Pinching out
If you want a bushy rather than a tall or
sprawling plant, pinch out the growing tips a
few times while it is still young. This will
stimulate the growth of sideshoots that will
produce a bushier effect. Most plants will
respond to this treatment, but beware of
doing it to slow-growing plants.

Holiday care

HOLIDAYS ARE GOOD FOR US, BUT NOT FOR PLANTS. UNLESS YOU HAVE A

FRIENDLY NEIGHBOUR WHO CAN PLANT-SIT FOR YOU, YOU WILL HAVE TO

DEVISE WAYS OF KEEPING YOUR PLANTS WATERED WHILE YOU ARE AWAY.

Short-term holiday care
If you have to leave your plants unattended for a while, try grouping them together in a large container. Place them on wet capillary matting and make sure the compost (potting soil) is moist too. If leaving them for more than a few days, you may need to arrange a system to keep the mat moist.

M ost houseplants will survive in winter for a few days, or even a week, if they are well watered beforehand, especially if the central heating is turned down. In hot summer weather, special arrangements will have to be made for your plants if you are leaving them for anything more than a long weekend.

If you can't arrange for a neighbour to pop in every couple of days to water your houseplants, take the following precautions:

- If it is summer, stand as many as possible outdoors. Choose a shady, sheltered position, and plunge the pots up to their rims in the soil. Then apply a thick mulch of chipped bark or peat over the pots to keep them cool and to conserve moisture. Provided that they are watered well before you leave, most plants will survive a week like this, even without rain.
- Move those that are too delicate to go outdoors into a few large groups in a cool position out of direct sunlight.
- Stand as many as possible on trays of gravel, watered to just below the level of the pot bases. Although this will not moisten the compost (potting soil), the humid air will help to keep the plants in good condition.
- Ensure that all of the most vulnerable plants have some kind of watering system.

Proprietary watering devices
Many kinds of watering devices can be bought, and new ones – usually variations on an old theme – appear each

year. Most work on one of the following principles:

Porous reservoirs are pushed into the compost (potting soil) and filled with water. The water slowly seeps though the porous walls over a period of a few days to a week. These are useful for one or two pots for a short period of time, but as you need one for each pot and the reservoir is small, their use is limited.

Ceramic mushrooms work on a similar principle, but the top is sealed and there is a connecting tube for insertion into a large reservoir of water (such as a bucket). As the water seeps through the porous shaft, the pressure in the sealed unit drops and fresh water is drawn from the reservoir. This simple but effective device will keep a plant happy for a couple of weeks, but again, you need one for each pot!

Wicks are sold for insertion into the base of the pot, which is then stood above a reservoir of water. This is a good method if you only have a handful of plants, otherwise too tricky to set up.

Drip feeds, sold for greenhouse and garden use, are a good solution. They can be expensive, and if you use a portable bag reservoir they are not very elegant for the home – but that will not matter while you are away.

Improvising
Two reliable systems use the kitchen sink or bath and capillary matting, which is available at all good garden centres and home improvement stores.

For the sink, cut a length of matting that fits the draining area and is

Improvised wicks
Make your own porous wicks by cutting capillary matting into strips. Make sure the wicks and compost (potting soil) are moist before you leave, and that the wick is pushed well into the compost.

Conserving moisture
Placing a plant in an inflated plastic bag like this will conserve the moisture for quite a long time, but if left too long there is a risk leaves rotting. Try to keep the bag out of contact with the leaves if possible.

g enough to dip into the basin part.
ɹ can fill this with water as a
ɾrvoir, or leave the plug out but let
 tap drip onto the mat to keep it
ịst. If you leave the tap dripping,
e a trial run beforehand to make
ẹ that it keeps the mat moist with-
 wasting water.

You can set up a similar arrangement in the bath, but if you want to
leave water in the bath, place the mat
and plants on a plank of wood supported on bricks, to leave space beneath for the water.

Bear in mind that compost (potting
soil) in clay pots with broken pots over

the drainage holes will not be able to
benefit from the capillary action effi-
ciently (though you could insert small
wicks though the holes, cut from
scraps of the matting). The system
works best for houseplants kept in
plastic pots, with nothing placed over
the drainage holes.

rdy plants
ny of the tougher houseplants can stand
doors with their pots plunged in the
und. Choose a shady spot, water the
nts thoroughly and cover the tops of the
s with a thick layer of chipped bark.

Porous irrigators
Porous irrigators can be useful if you only
leave your plants for a few days. Make sure
the compost (potting soil) is moist, then fill
the irrigators with water.

Porous wicks
Use a large needle to pull the wicks through
the compost (potting soil) and out of the
drainage hole at the base of the pot.

Ceramic mushrooms
Ceramic mushrooms can be very effective. As
water seeps through the porous container the
pressure drops, and more water is sucked up
from the reservoir. Provided the reservoir is
large enough, you should be able to leave
your plant for a week or more.

Using the bath
The bath is a good place to keep plants moist
on capillary matting; you can also stand the
plants on *porous* bricks without the mat.
Have a trial run to make sure the plug retains
the water without seepage.

Hydroculture

HYDROCULTURE – ALSO KNOWN AS HYDROPONICS – IS A METHOD OF
GROWING PLANTS WITHOUT SOIL OR COMPOST (POTTING SOIL). WATERING IS
NORMALLY ONLY NECESSARY EVERY COUPLE OF WEEKS, AND FEEDING IS ONLY
A TWICE-YEARLY TASK. HYDROCULTURE WILL GIVE YOU SUCCESSFUL PLANTS
WITH THE MINIMUM OF ATTENTION.

1. Choose a young plant and wash the root
free of all traces of compost (potting soil),
being careful not to damage them. Then
place the plant in a container with slatted or
mesh sides.

Hydroponics can be a highly scientific way to cultivate plants, with nutrient solutions carefully controlled by expensive monitoring equipment. However, the system usually used in homes by amateurs – and generally referred to as hydroculture – is designed to be simple and can be used successfully even by the complete beginner.

You can buy plants that are already growing hydroponically, and these are the best way to start as you would in any case have to buy suitable containers, clay granules and a special fertilizer. But once you realize how easy hydroculture plants are to look after, you will probably want to start off your own plants from scratch.

Routine care

Wait until the water indicator registers minimum, *but do not water immediately*. Allow an interval of two or three days before filling again. Don't keep topping up the water to keep it near the maximum level – it is important that air is allowed to penetrate to the lower levels.

Always use *tap* water because the special ion-exchange fertilizer depends on the chemicals in tap water to function effectively.

Make sure that the water is at room temperature. Because there is no compost (potting soil), cold water has an immediate chilling effect on the plant, and this is a common cause of failure with hydroculture plants.

HOW HYDROCULTURE WORKS

Plants can grow different kinds of roots: ground roots and water roots. If you root a cutting in water it will produce water roots, but once you pot it into compost (potting soil) it almost has to start again by producing ground roots. This makes the transition between compost and water cultivation tricky in either direction. But once the plant has passed through the transitional phase, a hydroculture plant can draw its moisture and nutrients from the solution at the base of the container, while those above can absorb the essential oxygen.

The level of the nutrient solution is crucial. If you fill the tank with too much water there will not be enough air spaces left for the roots to absorb sufficient oxygen and the plant will die.

5. Pack with more clay granules to secure
the inner pot and water indicator.

Make a note of when you replace the fertilizer, and renew it every six months. Some systems use the fertilizer in a 'battery' fitted within the special hydroculture pot, but otherwise you can just sprinkle it on to be washed in with a little water.

Just like plants in compost, hydroculture plants gradually grow larger. Because the roots do not have to

search for moisture and nutrients th
root system is usually smaller than fo
a comparable plant in compost, but i
time the plant will need repotting
especially if the top growth looks ou
of proportion with the container.

Remove the plant as carefully a
possible. It may be necessary to cu
the inner container to minimize dam
age to the roots, but sometimes yo
can leave the plant in the inner con
tainer and just use a larger outer one
If a very large and tangled root syster
has formed, some judicious prunin
may be called for. Both roots and to
growth can often be trimmed bac

Pack expanded clay granules around the ts, being careful to damage them as little ossible.

3. Insert the inner pot into a larger, watertight container, first placing a layer of clay granules on the base to raise the inner pot to the correct level of about 1cm (½in) below the rim.

4. Insert the water level tube. If you cannot find one specially designed to indicate the actual water level, use one that indicates how moist the roots are – those designed for other systems using aggregates are suitable.

Sprinkle the special hydroculture fertilizer er the clay granules.

7. Wash the fertilizer down as you water to the maximum level on the indicator. If the indicator does not show an actual level, add a volume of water equal to one-quarter the capacity of the container – and only water again when the indicator shows dry. Always fill with tap water.

8. A few months on and the houseplant is flourishing.

ccessfully, but much depends on e type of plant.

itable plants
ot all plants respond well to hydro-
lture, so some experimentation may
necessary. The range is surprisingly
de, however, and includes cacti and
cculents (with these it is essential to
sure an adequate 'dry period' before
pping up with more water, and not
let the water level rise too high), as
ll as orchids.
As a starting point, try some plants
m the following list, or be guided
what you see planted in

commercially-produced hydroculture units. Then experiment further as you gain more experience – *Aechmea fasciata*, aglaonema, amaryllis, anthurium, asparagus, aspidistra, beaucarnea, *Begonia manicata*, *Begonia rex*, cacti*, cissus, clivia, codiaeum, dieffenbachia, dizygotheca, dracaena, *Euphorbia pulcherrima*, ficus, gynura, hedera, hibiscus, hoya, maranta, monstera, nephrolepis, philodendron,

saintpaulia, sansevieria, schefflera, *Spathiphyllum wallisii*, stephanotis, streptocarpus, tradescantia, *Vriesea splendens*, yucca.

* Most cacti can be grown hydroponically, but it is essential that the water level is regulated carefully. If the water level is too high the plants will soon die.

Simple multiplication

A PLANT THAT YOU HAVE RAISED YOURSELF, FROM SEED OR A CUTTING, ALWAYS SEEMS MORE SPECIAL THAN ONE THAT YOU HAVE BOUGHT. PROPAGATION IS ONE OF THE MOST DEEPLY SATISFYING ASPECTS OF GARDENING, AND ONCE YOU HAVE ENOUGH PLANTS FOR YOUR OWN NEEDS YOU WILL STILL HAVE PLENTY TO EXCHANGE WITH FRIENDS.

Growing from seed

IT CAN BE PARTICULARLY GRATIFYING TO TELL ADMIRING FRIENDS THAT
YOU RAISED YOUR ABUTILON OR VENUS FLY TRAP FROM SEED, BUT PEREN-
NIALS CAN BE QUITE A CHALLENGE AND, IN THE CASE OF MIXTURES, NOT
ALL THE PLANTS WILL BE AS GOOD AS NAMED VARIETIES. ANNUALS, ON THE
OTHER HAND, ARE VERY EASY TO GROW AND SELDOM DISAPPOINT.

If you haven't grown housepla
from seed before, start with e
annuals, which will bring quick a
reliable results. This spurs most peo
to try the trickier or more interest
plants like cacti, cycads and fe
(which are actually grown from spo
and not true seeds), as well as favo
ites like saintpaulias.

As a general rule, those houspla
offered by seed merchants that nor
ally deal in the more common a
'everyday' plants are likely to be

How to sow in a tray

1. Fill the tray loosely with a seed compost
(medium) – loam- and peat-based (peat-moss
based) are equally satisfactory for the
majority of seeds. Do not use a potting
compost as the higher level of nutrients these
contain can inhibit germination.

2. Level off the compost, using a piece of
wood or rigid cardboard, then firm it gently
with a 'presser' or piece of wood that will fit
within the tray. Make sure that the compost is
still level.

3. Sprinkle the seeds as carefully and as
evenly as possible over the surface. A goo
way to do this with small seeds is in a fold
piece of paper that you tap gently with a
finger as you move it over the surface.

4. Unless the seed is very fine, or the packet
says that the seeds should be left exposed to
light, sprinkle a little more compost over the
top of the seeds. As a guide, cover with a
layer of compost that is about the thickness
of the seeds themselves. Use an old kitchen
sieve to sift the compost over. This keeps
back large pieces and makes it easier to
spread evenly.

5. Water carefully, using a watering-can
fitted with a very fine rose (fine-mist head) –
take the tray outdoors to do this. Otherwise
stand it in a bowl of water as described for
pots opposite. Place the tray in a propagator,
or cover it with a sheet of glass. Follow the
instructions on the seed packet regarding the
required level of light or darkness, and
temperature.

SOWING VERY
FINE SEED

Some seeds are very tiny, almos
like dust, making them difficult to
sow evenly. Mix seed that is this
small with a little silver sand in the
palm of one hand, then use the fing
and thumb of the other to sprinkle
the mixture over the surface of your
seed tray. If the seed and sand have
been well combined, distribution o
the seed should be even, especially
the sand will help you judge how
evenly you are sowing the seed.

iest to grow. Those offered by seed 'rchants specializing in the uncom- 'n or unusual are often more diffi- t to germinate, but the very fact t they are demanding explains part their appeal to many enthusiasts.

Many perennial houseplants can be w to germinate and they may take a iple of years to reach a respectable e. If you have a heated greenhouse conservatory it makes sense to grow m on in there until they are large bugh to be used for indoor display. Sow in trays if you need a lot of nts, otherwise use pots, as these e up less space.

cking out

soon as the seedlings are large ugh to handle, prick them out, ler into individual pots or into seed ys, to grow on until large enough their own pots.

Jse a potting compost (medium) for s, and always lift the seedlings efully by their leaves rather than by fragile stem.

AVOID THE CONDENSATION PROBLEM

Condensation will form inside a ropagator or on the sheet of glass overing the tray or pot. If this is so eavy that drips start to fall on the erminating seedlings, ventilate the ropagator or wipe the glass.

How to sow in a pot

1. Fill the pot with a seed compost (medium), but this time use a round presser to firm and level it gently. Make a presser from wood, or simply use a jam-jar.

3. Water by the immersion method. Stand the pot in a bowl of water, making sure that the water level remains below the top of the compost. Remove the pot to drain once the surface of the compost has become moist. Using this method, even the smallest seeds will not be disturbed.

2. Sow the seeds as evenly as possible. The easiest way to sow over the small area of a pot is to sprinkle the seeds between finger and thumb, as you might sprinkle salt. Sprinkle more compost over the sown seeds unless they are very fine, or the instructions on the packet advise otherwise. Most seeds should be covered with approximately their own depth of compost.

4. Place in a propagator or cover with a sheet of glass.

HT: Exacum affine *is one of the easiest eplants to try raising from seed. Sow in ng to flower in summer and autumn, or utumn to flower the following spring.*

Stem cuttings

MOST HOUSEPLANTS CAN BE RAISED FROM STEM CUTTINGS, AND SOME ARE SO

EASY THAT THEY WILL EVEN ROOT IN WATER. OTHERS ARE MORE CHALLENG-

ING, REQUIRING ROOTING HORMONES AND A PROPAGATOR.

Impatiens
Impatiens are often grown from seed, but
they root readily from softwood cuttings. As

old plants often lose their compact shape,
take a few cuttings periodically.

Geraniums
Geranium (pelargonium) softwood cuttings
root readily. You can use this technique for

zonal geraniums, regal geraniums like these,
and scented-leaved geraniums.

Most houseplants can be pr
agated from softwood cutti
taken in spring, and many of
shrubby plants root from semi-r
cuttings taken later in the year.

Softwood cuttings
This method of taking cuttings
similar to semi-ripe cuttings,
choose the ends of new shoots. T
softwood cuttings after the first fl
of spring but before the shoots h
become hard. Now follow the sa
procedure as for semi-ripe cuttings

Cuttings in water
Softwood cuttings can often be roc
in water, especially easy ones
coleus and impatiens.

Almost fill a jam-jar with water
fold a piece of wire-netting (chic
wire) over the top, or use a piece
aluminium foil with holes pierced
it. Take the cuttings in the nor
way but, instead of inserting th
into compost (potting soil), rest th
on the netting or foil, with the en
the stem in water.

Top up the water as necess
When roots have formed, pot the
tings up into individual pots usir
sandy potting compost. Keep
plants out of direct sunlight fo
least a week to give them a chanc
become established in the pot.

HORMONES
HELP ROOTING

Some plants, such as impatiens
and some tradescantias, root readil
even without help from a rooting
hormone. Others, and especially
semi-ripe cuttings, will benefit fro
the use of a rooting hormone.
Rooting hormones are available as
powders or liquids, and their use
usually results in more rapid rootin
and, in the case of the trickier kind
of plants, a higher success rate.

ow to take semi-ripe cuttings

Fill a pot with a cuttings compost edium) or use a seed compost, and firm it remove large pockets of air.

2. Make the cuttings 10–15cm (4–6in) long (they may have to be shorter on very compact plants), choosing the current season's growth after the first flush of growth but before the whole shoot has become hard. They should be firm yet flexible, and offer some resistance when bent.

3. Trim the cutting just below a leaf joint, using a sharp knife, and remove the lower leaves to produce a clear stem to insert into the compost.

Dip the cut end of the cutting into a ɔting hormone. If using a powder, moisten ǝ end in water first so that it adheres.

5. Make a hole in the compost with a small dibber or a pencil, and insert the cutting so that the bottom leaves are just above the compost. Firm the compost gently around the stem to remove large air pockets. You can usually insert several cuttings around the edge of a pot.

6. Water the cuttings (adding a fungicide to the water will help to reduce the risk of the cuttings rotting), then label and place in a propagator. If you don't have a propagator, cover the pot with a clear plastic bag, making sure it does not touch the leaves. Keep in a light place, but *out of direct sunlight*.

If a lot of condensation forms, reverse the bag or ventilate the propagator until excess condensation ceases to form. Do not allow the compost to dry out.

Pot up the cuttings individually once they have formed a good root system.

Leaf cuttings

LEAF CUTTINGS ALWAYS SEEM MORE FASCINATING TO ROOT THAN STEM CUTTINGS, AND THERE ARE PLENTY OF HOUSEPLANTS THAT YOU CAN PROPAGATE THIS WAY. THE TECHNIQUES ARE EASY AS WELL AS FUN, AND SOME OF THE MOST POPULAR PLANTS, SUCH AS SAINTPAULIAS, FOLIAGE BEGONIAS, STREPTOCARPUS AND SANSEVIERIAS, CAN BE RAISED FROM LEAF CUTTINGS.

Square leaf cuttings

1. First cut the leaf into strips about 3cm (1¼in) wide, in the general direction of the main veins, using a sharp knife or razor-blade

There are several types of leaf cuttings described here. For leaf petiole cuttings you need to remove the leaves with a length of stalk attached. Some leaves form new plants from the leaf blades, especially from points where the veins have been injured. For square leaf cuttings, instead of placing a whole leaf on the compost (medium), you can cut it into squares and insert these individually. With leaf midrib cuttings, the long, narrow leaves of plants such as streptocarpus can simply be sliced into sections and treated like square leaf cuttings.

Leaf petiole cuttings

1. Use only healthy leaves that are mature but not old. Remove the leaf with about 5cm (2in) of stalk, using a sharp knife or razorblade.

2. Fill a tray or pot with a suitable rooting compost (medium), then make a hole with dibber or pencil.

PLANTS TO GROW FROM LEAF CUTTINGS

🌿 **Leaf petiole cuttings**
Begonias (other than *B. rex*)
Peperomia caperata
Peperomia metallica
Saintpaulia

🌿 **Leaf blade cuttings**
Begonia rex

🌿 **Leaf midrib cuttings**
Gesneria
Sansevieria*
Sinningia speciosa (gloxinia)
Streptocarpus

* If you use this method for the variegated *S. trifasciata* 'Laurentii' the plantlets will not be variegated.

3. Insert the stalk into the hole, angling the cutting slightly, then press the compost gently around the stalk to firm it in. The base of the blade of the leaf should sit on the surface of the compost. You should be able to accommodate a number of cuttings in a seed tray or large pot. Water well, preferably with a fungicide, and allow surplus moisture to drain.

4. Place the cuttings in a propagator, or cover with a clear plastic bag. Make sure the the leaves do not touch the glass or plastic, and remove condensation periodically.
   Keep the cuttings warm and moist, in a light place out of direct sunlight. Young plan usually develop within a month or two, but leave them until they are large enough to be handled easily.

. Next cut across the strips to form small squares of leaf.

3. Fill a tray with a rooting compost (medium), then insert the squares on edge, making sure that the edge that was nearest to the leaf stalk faces downwards.

4. After a month or two you should have plenty of young plants that have grown from the leaf squares. Once these are well established, pot them up individually.

eaf midrib cuttings

. Remove a healthy, undamaged leaf from
e parent plant, ideally one that has only
cently fully expanded.

LONGITUDINAL LEAF CUTTINGS

An alternative method of propagating streptocarpus:

Lay the leaf on a hard surface, and cut it twice along the length of the leaf, on both sides of the main vein. Discard the main vein.

Insert these halves into the compost, so that they stand on edge with about one-third in the compost.

2. Place the leaf face down on a firm, clean surface, such as a sheet of glass. Cut the leaf into strips, no wider than 5cm (2in).

3. Fill a tray or large pot with a rooting compost (medium), and insert the cuttings into this about 2.5cm (1in) apart. Insert the end that was nearest the stalk into the compost. About one-third of the cutting should be in the compost.

Young plants will eventually appear from the compost. Pot these up individually when they are large enough to handle safely.

Leaf blade cuttings

1. Select a healthy leaf, and sever it close to the base of the main stalk.

2. Cut off the attached stalk close to the blade.

3. Cut across the main and secondary veins on the underside of the leaf, using a sharp knife or razor-blade. Make the cuts about 2.5cm (1in) apart.

4. Fill a seed tray with a rooting compost (medium), then peg the leaf so that the back is in contact with the compost. Make several small U-shaped 'staples' from pieces of galvanized wire, to act as anchors.

5. Alternatively, instead of using wire staples, you can hold the leaf in contact with the compost by using small stones as weights.

6. Keep in a propagator, or in a warm place, in a light position but out of direct sunlight. Do not allow the compost to become dry.

New plants will eventually grow, and once these look well established, pot them up individually. Often the old leaf has disintegrated by this time, but if not, just cut the new plants free of the old leaf.

LEFT: Begonia rex *should be propagated using leaf-blade cuttings, rather than other methods.*

Easy division

DIVISION IS THE QUICKEST AND EASIEST OF ALL METHODS OF PROPAGATION.

THE RESULTS ARE INSTANT, AND MOST PLANTS WITH A CROWN OR THAT

FORM A CLUMP CAN BE PROPAGATED THIS WAY.

Many ferns can be divided, including adiantum, phyllitis, and *Pteris cretica*. Marantas, and related genera such as calathea, also form a clump and lend themselves to division. Other popular houseplants to try are anthuriums and aspidistras.

Water the plant about an hour before you divide it. If the roots are thick and fleshy, have a sharp knife handy to cut though them.

Dividing a plant

Knock the plant out of its pot. If the plant large and the pot full of roots, you may ed to invert the pot and tap the rim on a rd surface. Place a hand over the root-ball catch it as it falls free.

2. Pull away some of the compost (potting soil) from the bottom and sides, freeing some of the roots in the process.

Try pulling the plant apart with your nds, first into two pieces, and then into naller ones if you need a lot of new plants.

4. Sometimes the tough or fleshy roots make this difficult: chlorophytums are an example. If this is the case, prise the roots apart with a hand fork and separate the clump into smaller pieces with a sharp knife.

5. Replant healthy young pieces of the root clump, using a smaller pot and a good potting compost (medium). It may be necessary to trim back some of the largest roots with a knife, but try to leave the small, fibrous ones intact.

After watering, keep the plants in good light but out of direct sun, at least until they have become established and started to grow again.

Layering

LAYERING IS A USEFUL TECHNIQUE IF YOU REQUIRE JUST A FEW EXTRA OR

REPLACEMENT PLANTS. ORDINARY LAYERING IS ONLY PRACTICAL FOR A FEW

PLANTS INDOORS, BUT AIR LAYERING IS A POPULAR WAY TO IMPROVE AN OLD

FICUS THAT HAS BECOME BARE AT THE BASE.

Ordinary layering is most appro
priate for climbers or trailers wit
long and flexible shoots that can easi
be pegged down into pots close to th
parent plant. Ivies and *Philodendr*
scandens are plants that readily len
themselves to this form of propagatior

Air layering is most often used fc
large ficus, such as *F. elastica*, but th
method can also be used for othe
plants, such as dracaenas. Normall
plants are air layered on an area of ba
stem just below the leafy part, but if
few old leaves are in the way cut thes
off flush with the stem.

Ordinary layering

1. Fill a few small pots with a seed or cuttings compost (medium), and position them close to the parent plant.

2. Choose long, healthy shoots with young growth, and untangle them from the rest of the plant so that they can be pegged down into the pots.

ABOVE: Philodendron scandens *is one of the few plants which you can successfully propagate by ordinary layering.*

3. Use pieces of bent wire to hold the stem in contact with the compost where there is a leaf joint. It does not matter if the stem is slightly covered by the compost.

4. When the roots have formed – usually after about four weeks – and new shoots begin to grow, sever the new plant from its parent. Keep the newly severed plant in a light position out of direct sunlight, and pay special attention to watering, until it is well established and obviously growing away strongly.

ABOVE: *Try air layering a leggy* Ficus elastica *'Robusta' and you will once more have a plant like this.*

ir layering

Make a sleeve out of a piece of clear astic and secure it below the point where e layer is to be made, using a plastic- overed twist-tie or adhesive tape. Then, sing a sharp knife or blade, make an oward-facing cut about 2.5cm (1in) long, ishing just below a leaf joint. Make sure at you do not cut more than about e-third of the way through the stem, herwise the top may break.

2. Brush inside the wound with a rooting hormone. A small paintbrush is useful for this. To hold the wound open, insert some moist sphagnum moss into the incision, or use a small piece of matchstick.

3. Pack plenty of moist sphagnum moss around the area, then bring up the plastic sleeve to hold it in place.

Secure the top of the sleeve with another vist-tie or some adhesive tape.

5. Check the moss occasionally to make sure that it is still moist, and to see if any roots have formed.

6. Once new roots are visible through the sleeve, cut off the stem just below the root-ball. Loosen the ball of moss slightly, but do not attempt to remove the moss when you pot up the plant. As the root system will still be small at this stage, it may be necessary to provide a stake for a few weeks.

Offsets and plantlets

OFFSETS AND PLANTLETS PROVIDE YOU WITH NEW PLANTS FOR THE MINIMUM

OF EFFORT – AND YOU DON'T HAVE TO SACRIFICE THE PARENT PLANT.

A few plants obligingly grow 'babies' on their leaves – just waiting to root when they come into contact with the compost (potting soil). Others produce plantlets on runners and raising new plants from these is as simple as pegging them down. Many plants – such as bromeliads – produce new shoots clustered around the old ones. These are easily detached and potted up.

Plantlets

Two succulents popularly grown as curiosities carry baby plants on their leaves: *Kalanchoe daigremontiana* (syn. *Bryophyllum daigremontianum*) and *K. Tubiflora* (syn. *B. tubiflorum*). The plantlets often fall off and can be found growing in the compost (potting soil) at the base of the parent plant. Just lift these up carefully after loosening the compost, and pot them up individually. Alternatively, re- move the largest of the plantlets from

the leaves before they fall, and gently press them into the surface of a cut- tings compost (medium). Other vivi- parous plants like this, such as *Asple- nium bulbiferum*, can be treated in the same way.

Tolmiea menziesii has young plant- lets at the base of its leaves. Just detach a parent leaf, cut off the sur- plus leaf blade around the plantlet, and bury it just below the compost, with the plantlet still visible.

Runners

Some popular houseplants, such as *Saxifraga stolonifera*, produce plantlets on long runners, others, like *Chlor- ophytum comosum*, produce them at the ends of arching stems. All of these are very easy to propagate.

Place small pots filled with a cut- tings compost (medium) around the parent plant and peg down the plant- lets into them using pieces of bent wire or hairpins, to hold them in close

1. Bromeliads produce offsets around the edge of the main flowering part of the plant, which later dies. Pot up these offsets when they are about a third the height of the parent plant.

contact with the compost. Keep we watered and sever the plantlets fro the parent plant once plenty of roc have formed and the new plant h started to grow.

Offsets

Some plants produce offsets – ne growth close to the old that can separated and grown on independent – and this is normal with bromeliad

Runners

1. *Chlorophytum comosum* is easy to propagate from plantlets produced at the ends of long, arching stems.

2. Peg the plantlets down into small pots, using pieces of bent wire to hold them in position.

3. Sever the plants from their parent once they have rooted well and are growing strongly.

, They can usually be pulled away easily, ut if necessary cut them away with a knife.

3. Pot the offsets up individually.

4. Firm the plants in, then water and keep in a warm, humid position, out of hot direct sunlight, until they show signs of new growth.

Many epiphytic bromeliads (those hat in nature grow in trees or on ocks) have flowering rosettes that die fter blooming. Before these plants ie, they produce plenty of offsets round the old mature rosette. Leave hese on until they are about one-third f the size of the parent plant, then etach them and pot up individually. lost can simply be pulled off by and, but the tough ones will have to e severed with a sharp knife.

Some terrestrial bromeliads, such as nanas, produce offsets on stolons short horizontal stems). Remove the lant from its container and cut off the ffsets without causing too much dam- ge to the parent.

Pot up the offsets without delay, nd keep moist. Position them in good ight but out of direct sunlight. They ill soon start to grow independently nd should then be treated normally.

Propagating from plantlets

1. *Kalanchoe tubiflora* (syn. *Bryophyllum tubiflorum*) produces plenty of plantlets at the ends of its leaves. Remove the plantlets with a gentle tug, and avoid holding the roots.

2. Plant them in a free-draining cuttings compost (medium), where they will soon grow away as young plants.

3. *Kalanchoe daigremontiana* (syn. *Bryophyllum daigremontianum*) produces plantlets around the edges of its leaves. Treat like the previous species, or simply peg down a whole leaf.

4. The ensuing plantlets can be potted up singly when they are larger.

Special techniques

SPECIAL TECHNIQUES LIKE CANE CUTTINGS, LEAF-BUD CUTTINGS, CACTI CUTTINGS AND CACTI GRAFTING ARE USEFUL SKILLS TO ACQUIRE. EVEN IF YOU DON'T USE THE METHODS OFTEN, THEY ARE INVALUABLE FOR PROPAGATING CERTAIN PLANTS.

S ome houseplants with thick and erect stems, such as cordylines, dracaenas and dieffenbachias, can be propagated by a technique known as cane cuttings. This is a good method to try if a plant has lost most of its leaves and you are left with a long length of bare stem. In this case, you might as well use the leggy shoots for cane cuttings.

Leaf-bud cuttings are sometimes used for *Ficus elastica*, especially where more plants are required than you could achieve with air layering. You can also use this method of propagation for *Aphelandra squarrosa*, dracaenas, epipremnums, *Monstera deliciosa* and philodendrons.

The majority of cacti will root fairly easily from cuttings, but their odd shapes, as well as their prickles, call for special techniques.

If the cactus has rounded pads (like opuntias), just cut new pads off making a straight cut across the joint. Leave the cutting exposed for about 48 hours for the wound to form a callus. Then insert the cutting into a mixture of grit or coarse sand and peat (peat moss) or peat substitute. Once the cutting has rooted and started to grow, pot it up into a normal cactus compost (medium).

Columnar cacti can often be propagated if the top 5–10cm (2–4in) of stem is removed. Dry off as described above, before inserting the cutting.

Flat-stemmed cacti such as epiphyllums can be cut into lengths about 5cm (2in) long. Dry off as usual then insert upright in the compost.

Cane cuttings

1. Cut the thick stem into pieces about 5–7.5cm (2–3in) long, making sure that each piece has at least one node (the area between two points where leaves were attached).

2. You can insert them vertically, but they are usually laid horizontally with the lower half pressed into the compost. Make sure that the leaf buds are pointing upwards.

Leaf-bud cuttings

1. Select a young stem in spring or summer and cut it into 1–2.5cm (½–1in) sections, each with one leaf and its bud.

BLEEDING WOUNDS

Some succulents, such as euphorbias, produce a milky latex when cut. If this happens, dip the cutting into tepid water for a few seconds to stop the flow. Hold a damp cloth over the cut surface on the parent plant to stop the bleeding. As the sap of some is an irritant, be careful not to get it near your eyes or on your skin.

HANDLING PRICKLY CACTI

Thick gloves make it possible to handle some spiny cacti while taking cuttings, as you do not have to grip the plant hard, but many will simply pierce the gloves. To handle these, fold a newspaper over several times to form a thick band a couple of centimetres (about an inch) wide, then grip the plant with this, holding the 'handles' formed by the ends. A flexible piece of cardboard can be used in a similar way, but be careful not to use anything so hard that the spines are damaged.

Dip the base of each cutting in a rooting ormone, then insert it in a 7.5cm (3in) pot ed with a cuttings compost (medium).

3. To reduce moisture loss from the leaf, curl the leaf so that it is rolled up, and hold in place with an elastic band. This also saves space as you can pack the pots closer together than if the leaves were spread horizontally.

4. Once roots have formed, often after about a month if you have used a propagator, remove the elastic band and give the plant more space. Pot on into a normal potting compost (medium) a few weeks later.

acti cuttings

Cacti and succulents like this are easy to ise from cuttings. Just remove a stem of itable length.

2. Leave the cutting exposed for about 48 hours to allow the wound to form a callus.

3. Insert the cuttings like those of any other plant. A rooting hormone should not be necessary.

Columnar cacti often have only a single em, so waiting for separate young shoots n be a problem. However, they can often e propagated if the top 5–10cm (2–4in) of e stem is removed. Allow the cut surface to ·y for 48 hours before inserting the cutting.

5. Cacti with flat pads are easy to root but need careful handling (see *Handling Prickly Cacti*, opposite). Treat as the other types, once removed.

6. These two cuttings have been taken from a columnar cactus (left) and one with flat pads (right).

Sometimes cacti are grafted for fun, or to make them flower more quickly than they would on their own roots, but a few that have stem colours other than green, such as some orange-red gymnocalycium species and varieties, have to be grafted onto a green stem because they are incapable of supporting themselves without the green chlorophyll found there. For these, flat grafting is the easiest method.

Some orchids, such as cymbidiums, have back-bulbs (a kind of bulb that sits on the surface of the compost). These can be removed and potted separately to produce new plants. Orchids can also be propagated using the division technique.

Fern spores can be used to propagate new plants; they resemble dust-like seeds, but they are not the equivalent of seeds. The fern plant is just an asexual stage in the life cycle, and the spores are another asexual stage. When they germinate they produce the sexual stage, the prothallus, which is green and prostrate or scale-like and carries both male and female organs. When fertilization takes place, the fern as we know it begins to grow.

Propagating orchids

1. Orchids can produce large clumps and may need dividing. Remove growth from th outer edge to repot. Some produce back-bulbs (old bulbs without leaves) that can be used for repotting.

2. Pot up individually, and always use a special orchid compost (medium). Back-bul (which may have no leaves) are treated in t same way. Plant to one side of the pot, as new growth will expand in front of the old growth.

Grafting cacti

1. Slice the top off the rootstock using a sharp knife to produce a flat surface.

2. Slightly bevel the edges of the cut with a knife.

3. Slice off the part to be grafted onto the rootstock, again cutting it cleanly.

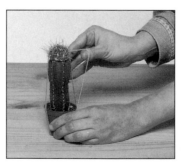

4. Place the two parts together and hold in place with a couple of elastic bands looped over the top of the grafted cacti and under the bottom of the pot.

5. Label and keep in a warm, light place. T elastic bands can be removed as soon as new growth is noticed. The grafted cactus o the left is *Gymnocalycium* 'Black Cap'.

rns from spores

Fill a shallow pot with a peaty compost at-moss potting soil). Some people then inkle a thin layer of brick dust over the . Firm it gently so that it is lightly npacted and level.

2. Sprinkle the spores over the surface as evenly as possible.

3. Cover the pot with a piece of glass and stand it in a saucer of water (rain or soft water is best). Keep in a warm, shaded position, and make sure that there is some water in the saucer.

LOW: *Fern spores are usually sold to ateurs as mixtures of either hardy or bical species. This* Asplenium nidus *is fern that a mixture might include, but if want to propagate a particular species it worth saving and sowing the spores from r own plants.*

4. In about a month the tiny prothalli will start to grow and gradually cover the surface. It is essential that the compost remains moist at this stage. It is also worth keeping the glass over the pot.

5. A month or two later the ferns proper should begin to appear. At this stage, remove the glass but still keep out of direct hot sunlight. When large enough to handle, prick out the little clumps of ferns into a seed tray.

When the small ferns are large enough to handle easily and a suitable size for their own pot, prick them out into individual pots.

Trouble-shooting

No matter how circumspect you are in selecting new plants, how carefully you check them for signs of ill-health, or how well you care for them, pests and diseases arrive unannounced. However, they should never be allowed to spoil your enjoyment of houseplants and with a little vigilance most should be easily kept under control.

Eliminating pests

EVERYONE GETS PESTS ON THEIR HOUSEPLANTS: BEGINNERS, EXPERTS AND

EVEN PROFESSIONALS. SOME, LIKE APHIDS, READILY ATTACK A WHOLE RANGE

OF PLANTS, OTHERS ARE MORE SELECTIVE AND TEND TO BE A PROBLEM ONLY

ON CERTAIN TYPES OF PLANT, OR IN PARTICULAR CONDITIONS. ALL NEED TO

BE DEALT WITH QUICKLY AND EFFECTIVELY.

Red spider mites
Red spider mites are so small that you can hardly see them without a magnifying glass, but, as this sick *Fatsia japonica* shows, an infestation can be serious.

Aphids
Aphids are perhaps the most common and troublesome pest, but are relatively easy to control provided you act as soon as they are detected.

Whitefly
Whitefly look like tiny white moths that often rise up like a cloud when the plant is moved. Although tiny, they gradually weaken the plant, as this radermachera shows.

Mealy bugs
Mealy bugs are slow-moving and multiply le rapidly than aphids, but they still weaken th plant and can spread diseases.

Most pests fall into one of the three categories given below, so even if you do encounter a pest that you don't immediately recognize, you should be able to decide from this information which group it falls in, and choose an appropriate control.

Sap-suckers

The ubiquitous aphids are the biggest problem, and even if you win the first battle when you realize that an attack is under way, never let your guard down because there will always be new armies of aphids to take their place.

Aphids, and all sap-sucking insects, are important not only for the immediate damage they do, but also because of the long-term health risk to your plants. When aphids cluster on buds or the tips of shoots, leaves and flowers will often be distorted when they open, and because they tap into

the veins and 'blood' supply of the plant, they can easily transmit virus diseases from one plant to another. Always take aphids seriously, and take action before the population rapidly increases, as they can reproduce at a phenomenal rate.

Whitefly look like tiny moths and rise up in a cloud when disturbed. The nymphs (immature insects) are green to white and scale-like, turning yellow before emerging as an adult fly.

Red spider mites are tiny and the actual insects are easily missed, but you will notice their fine webs and yellowing, mottled leaves.

Control: almost all houseplant insecticides will control aphids, so choose one that is convenient to use, and has the right persistence taking into account your personal views on garden chemicals. You can buy some insecti-

cides that kill only aphids and lea beneficial insects unharmed, but the home this is of marginal benef You don't have to worry about pol nating insects or natural predators you might outdoors. Many strong i secticides are not suitable for use i doors, but you can take your pla outside to spray it. Alternatively, u one of the milder and less persiste ones – often based on natural subs ances like pyrethrum – more often.

Systemic insecticides that you w ter into the soil, or that are contain in impregnated sticks pushed into t compost, are easy to use indoors a protect the plant for weeks.

Pests like whitefly need repeat spraying with ordinary contact inse ticides, so don't give up too soon.

Red spider mites dislike a hum atmosphere. Once you've used t chemical control, regular misting

Caterpillar damage
Caterpillars can be a problem on indoor plants as well as in the garden. Here one has attacked a pereskia.

Biological controls
A predatory mite – *Phytoseiulus persimilis* – can be used for red spider mite as a biological control. Here a leaf containing the parasite is being placed on a houseplant.

Nematode weevil control
There is now a natural control for vine weevil grubs – a microscopic parasitic nematode. Mix the culture with water and apply to the plants. Here a cyclamen is being dosed.

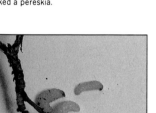

Vine weevil grubs
Vine weevil grubs are particularly troublesome because they eat the roots and at first you may know of the problem is when the plant collapses.

Using systemic insecticides
These special 'pins' release a systemic insecticide that is absorbed by the plant's roots, making the plant toxic to sap-sucking insects for weeks.

Controlling aphids
You may be able to reduce the population of insects such as aphids simply by swishing the plant in water.

create a humid atmosphere will please the plants and deter the mites.

Mealy bugs and other relatively stationary sap-sucking insects can be treated by dabbing them with a cotton swab dipped in alcohol. This will penetrate the waxy coat that protects them from most contact insecticides. Otherwise try using a systemic insecticide that will be carried in the sap.

Leaf eaters
Leaf eaters give themselves away soon after arrival, by the tell-tale chunks missing from leaves. Fortunately, most of the these pests are large and easily seen, and on the whole control is relatively simple.

Control: large pests that remain on the plant, such as caterpillars, slugs and snails, can usually be picked off by hand (remove the whole leaf if in-

fested). Chemical control is hardly ever necessary indoors, but in a conservatory you may want to use slug bait (protect it under pieces of broken pot if you have pets).

Those insects that feed at night and hide during the day, such as earwigs, present a bigger problem. Most household crawling insect powders and sprays will control these if you use them around the area where the plants are. If you don't want to use an insecticide, leave small traps made from matchboxes, left slightly open and filled with litter such as chopped straw. Check these each morning and destroy any pests that you find.

Root chewers
The problem with root pests is that you are unlikely to know of their existence until the plant collapses, by which time it's often too late.

A number of pests affect the roots, from some types of aphids to the grubs of insects such as weevils. If a plant looks sick, fails to grow properly, or starts to collapse, and there is no obvious cause such as overwatering or underwatering, remove the plant from its pot and shake off the compost (potting soil). Examine the roots: if there are grubs or other pests, that's the likely cause; if you find none but the roots are sparse or rotting, a fungus disease is the more likely cause.

Control: if you have taken the plant out of its pot for examination, shake the compost off the roots and dip them into an insecticidal solution before repotting in fresh compost. Your plant may then recover. Drench the compost in nearby pots with an insecticidal solution as a further precaution, though results may be variable.

Dealing with diseases

PLANT DISEASES CAN BE DISFIGURING AND EVEN FATAL, SO ALWAYS TAKE THEM SERIOUSLY. IF YOU CAN'T CONTROL THEM BY PICKING OFF THE AFFECTED LEAVES, RAPID RESORT TO A FUNGICIDE MAY BE THE BEST SOLUTION. IF A VIRUS STRIKES, IT MAY BE BETTER TO SACRIFICE THE PLANT TO THE BIN RATHER THAN RISK THE INFECTION SPREADING TO OTHER PLANTS.

Fungus diseases are often difficult to identify accurately and many different species of fungi can cause similar symptoms. Fortunately, a scientific identification of the exact fungus is not necessary in order to go about controlling it. The chemicals used to control each main group of diseases are largely effective against all the organisms likely to be responsible – but don't assume that all fungicides are equally effective against all fungus diseases. Always read the label to check what disease a particular chemical is most effective against.

Leaf spots
Various fungi and bacteria cause leaf spots. If tiny black specks can be seen on the affected surface, they are likely to be the spore-bearing bodies of a fungus, so a fungicide is likely to be effective. If no specks can be detected it might be a bacterial problem, though a fungicide might still be of some help.

Leaf spot
Leaf spots are quite common, and are caused by various fungi. If just a few leaves are affected, pick them off then spray the rest of the plant as a precaution.

Control: prune off and destroy affected leaves. Water with a systemic fungicide, and avoid misting too frequently. Increase ventilation if weather permits.

Root rots
The first sign of a root rot is usually the sudden collapse of a seemingly healthy plant. The leaves turn brown or black, and curl up. The entire plant may wilt. This is almost always result of overwatering.

Control: if the plant has not already deteriorated too far, try drying it out. However, there is usually little that can be done at this stage.

Sooty mould
The fungus covers the leaves, often on back but sometimes the front, with black growth that looks like soot. does not directly harm the plants looks unsightly.

Fungal diseases
The protective sleeve of this newly purchased saintpaulia disguised the fact that it is infected with *Botrytis cinerea*. This grey-brown mould develops on dead or damaged plants, and can be caused by lack of ventilation.

ty mould

ty mould is a fungus that grows on the
ary substance excreted by aphids and
er sap-suckers. If you control the pests
will eliminate the disease, which is
ghtly but not particularly harmful.

Mildew

Various kinds of mildew affect houseplants,
and begonias are particularly prone to them.
Control is difficult once the disease is well
established, but various fungicides are useful
for early and preventative treatment.

ntrol: sooty mould is a fungus that
es on the 'honeydew' (excrement)
: by aphids and whitefly. When
s food disappears so will the sooty
uld, so eliminate the insects that
the prime cause.

dews

ere are various kinds of mildew, the
wdery types being the most com-
n. Evidence of the disease is seen as
hite, powdery deposit, almost as if
leaf has been sprinkled with flour.
e problem starts in one or two areas
: quickly radiates out and can soon
gulf the whole leaf. Some plants,
h as begonias, are more prone to
dew than others.

ntrol: pick off the affected leaves at
early stage, then use a fungicide to
it its spread. Increase ventilation,
d reduce the humidity around the
nt — at least until the disease is
der control.

Using fungicides

If you need to use a fungicide, you can use
those developed for outdoor plants by mixing
a small amount and using it in a hand-
pumped mister.

Viruses

The main symptoms of virus diseases
are stunted or distorted growth,
irregular yellow blotches on foliage
and streaked petals on flowering
plants. They are easily transmitted by
sap-sucking insects such as aphids,
and can even be carried on the knives
used to take cuttings.

There is no effective control and,
apart from the rare cases where the
plants are cultivated for the variegation caused by the virus, the plants are
best destroyed.

Disorders and deficiencies

NOT ALL TROUBLES ARE CAUSED BY PESTS AND DISEASES. SOMETIMES PHY-

SIOLOGICAL PROBLEMS SUCH AS CHILLS AND COLD DRAUGHTS, OR NUTRI-

TIONAL DEFICIENCIES, CAN BE THE CAUSE.

Tracking down a physiological problem calls for a bit of detective work. The descriptions of some common problems described here will help to pinpoint some potential causes, but be prepared to look for anything that has disturbed the usual routine – has the plant been moved, watered more or less heavily, has the weather become much colder, have you turned the central heating on but not increased humidity or ventilation? By piecing together the various clues you can often deduce probable causes, and thereby work out what you can do to avoid a repetition.

Temperature
Most houseplants will tolerate cool but frost-free temperatures if they have to. It is sudden changes of temperature or icy draughts in a warm room that cause most problems.

If leaves drop it may be due to low temperature. This often happens with newly bought plants that have been on display outdoors or chilled on the way home. Leaves that look shrivelled and slightly translucent may have been touched by frost.

Hardy plants like *Euonymus japonicus* may drop their leaves if kept too warm in winter. Berries are also likely to fall prematurely if the temperature is kept too high.

Light and sun
Plants that need a high light intensity will become elongated and drawn if the illumination is poor, and leaves and flower stalks will be drawn towards the window. Lop-sided growth is another indication of inadequate

Neglect
This plant is clearly showing signs of stress and lack of nutrients. It may be best to discard a plant in this state.

Sun scorch
Plants that are not adapted to grow in very strong light are easily scorched by strong sunlight intensified by a glass window. This dieffenbachia is suffering from scorch.

light. If you can't move the plant i a lighter position, try turning the round by 45 degrees each day (pu tiny mark on the pot as a reminde whether you've turned it).

Light is usually a good thing, I direct sunlight, intensified throu glass, will often scorch leaves – effect will be brown, papery areas the leaf. Patterned glass is a particu problem as it can act like a magnify glass, causing dry brown patc where the rays have been concentrat

Humidity
Dry air can cause leaf tips to go bro and papery on vulnerable plants.

Watering
Too little water is the most lik cause of wilting and collapse, if compost (potting soil) feels very dry the touch. If the plant collapses a the compost feels very wet, or wate standing in the saucer or cache-p suspect overwatering.

Feeding
Pale leaves and short, stunted grow may be due to lack of fertilizer in

Effects of overwatering
Yellowing lower leaves are often a sign of overwatering, but may also be due to a ch it happens in winter. This is a *Fatshedera l* beginning to show signs of overwatering.

ᵃrosol scorch
ᵖlant can also be damaged by aerosol
ᵖays (even one containing an insecticide
ᵗended for houseplants). This dieffenbachia
ᵃs dropped many of its leaves, and others
ᵉ scorched, because an insecticidal aerosol
ᵃs used too close to the plant.

Effects of dry air
Dry air is a particular problem for most ferns.
This adiantum is showing the signs of low
humidity.

ᵒmpost (potting soil). Try liquid
ᵉding for a quick boost. Specific
ᵃnts, such as citrus fruits and rho-
dendrons, may show signs of iron
ᵈficiency (yellowing leaves) if grown
ᵃn alkaline compost. Feed with a
ᵉlated (sequestered) iron and next
ᵐe you repot use an ericaceous com-
ˢt (specially developed for lime-
ᵗing plants).

ᵘd drop
ᵘd drop is often caused by dry com-
ˢt (potting soil) or dry air, but
ᵐetimes it is due to the plant being
ᵒved to a different position or turned
ᵈce the buds have formed. (Zygocac-
ˢ is an example of a plant that
ᵉents having to re-orientate its buds
ᵗ light from a different direction.)

Dehydration
This thunbergia shows the classic symptoms
of a dehydrated plant. The very dry compost
(potting soil) is confirmation of the cause. The
best treatment is to stand the pot in a bowl
of water for several hours, until the compost
is thoroughly wet. Peat (peat moss) composts
are particularly difficult to rewet once they
have dried out completely, but a few drops of
mild household detergent added to the water
will help to rewet it.

Bud drop
Bud drop is often caused by dry root,
overwatering, or by moving a plant once the
flower buds have formed.

Wilting and worse

WHEN A PLANT WILTS OR APPEARS TO COLLAPSE, IT'S TIME TO TAKE DRASTIC ACTION. THE FIRST PRIORITY IS TO DECIDE WHAT'S WRONG, THEN, IF POSSIBLE, TO APPLY FIRST AID MEASURES WITHOUT DELAY TO BRING THE PLANT BACK TO HEALTH.

First aid for a dry plant

1. If the leaves of a plant have started to wilt like this, the compost (potting soil) is probably too dry. Feel it first – overwatering also causes wilting.

2. Stand the pot in a bowl or bucket of water and leave it until the air bubbles have ceased to rise.

3. It will take some hours for the water to revive the plant. In the meantime, help the plant further by misting the leaves with water from time to time.

4. Once the plant has revived, remove it from the bowl and stand it in a cool place out of direct sunlight for at least a day.

Wilting and collapse are a sign that something is drastically wrong. If you ignore this warning you may lose the plant. Plants usually wilt for one of three reasons:

- Too much water.
- Too little water.
- Insects or a disease affecting the roots.

The first two will usually be obvious: if the compost (potting soil) is hard and dry, underwatering is the likely cause: if there is water standing in the cache-pot or saucer, or if the compost oozes water, overwatering is almost certainly the cause.

If the compost seems neither overwatered nor underwatered, check the base of the plant just above compost level. If the stem looks black or rotten, a fungus disease is the likely cause and the plant is best discarded.

If none of the above symptoms are present, remove the plant from its pot and shake off some of the soil. If many of the roots are soft or black and decaying, a root disease is the likely cause. Look also for grubs or other insects around the roots. The larvae of beetles such as weevils can sometimes cause a plant to collapse.

First aid for root pests or disease
It will be very difficult to revive a plant with a severe root rot, but you can try drenching the compost with fungicide, then after a couple of hours letting it dry out on absorbent paper. If the root system is badly damaged it may be worth repotting it in sterilized compost first, after removing as much of the old soil as possible.

Some soil pests, such as root aphids, can be controlled if drenched with insecticide. Wine weevil grubs and other serious soil pests are not so easy to control. Try shaking the old soil off the roots, dusting them with an insecticidal powder, then repotting in fresh, sterilized compost. If the damage is not too extensive the plant may survive once it has had time to make new growth.

rst aid for a wet plant

Knock the plant out of its pot. If it does
: come out easily, invert the plant while
ding the compost (potting soil) in with one
d, and knock the rim of the pot on a hard
ace.

2. Wrap the root-ball in several layers of
absorbent paper.

3. Stand the plant in a warm place, out of
direct sunlight, with more absorbent paper
wrapped around the root-ball. Change the
paper periodically if it is still drawing
moisture from the compost.

OTHER POSSIBLE CAUSES OF COLLAPSE

Plants may collapse for
hysiological reasons:

Cold air at night, especially in
inter, may cause some plants to
ollapse, especially if they have been
ept warm during the day.

Strong, hot sunshine through
lass will make many plants wilt.
Jsually they recover when given
ooler, shadier conditions.

Hot, dry air will have a similar
ffect on some plants, such as the
nore delicate ferns.

Poor light will eventually cause a
lant to exhaust itself. But this is
ikely to be a gradual process, much
ess rapid than collapse caused by
vatering problems or pests.

4. Continue until the compost has
dried out, but do not let it become
completely dry. Repot and water
only very cautiously for the next week.

Creative displays

WHETHER YOU COLLECT HOUSE-PLANTS AS A PHILATELIST COLLECTS STAMPS, OR WHETHER YOU CHOOSE THEM IN THE SAME WAY AS AN INTERIOR DESIGNER SELECTS A PAINTING, YOU HAVE TO FIND POSITIONS THAT WILL NOT ONLY PLEASE THE PLANT, BUT ALSO SUIT THE DÉCOR.

Interior design

THE WAY IN WHICH YOU FURNISH AND DECORATE YOUR HOME IS AN EXPRESSION OF YOUR OWN PERSONALITY. YOU MAY NOT BE ABLE TO INFLUENCE THE WORLD OUTSIDE, OR EVEN YOUR WORKPLACE, BUT IN YOUR OWN HOME YOU CAN MAKE THE KIND OF STATEMENTS THAT PLEASE YOU PERSONALLY. HOUSEPLANTS CAN HELP YOU TO CREATE YOUR CHOSEN IMAGE: WHETHER WARM AND 'COTTAGEY', BOLD AND CLINICAL, STYLISH AND ELEGANT, OR SIMPLY PROVOCATIVE. IT DOES NOT MATTER WHETHER YOU HAVE A COUNTRY COTTAGE, CITY FLAT, OR SUBURBAN HOUSE, YOU CAN USE PLANTS TO COMPLEMENT YOUR CHOSEN DÉCOR.

A room without plants is rather like a meal without any seasoning. It serves its purpose and can even look good, but it lacks spice and that extra ingredient that would make it interesting. Not everyone wants to be strangled by an over-exuberant ivy as they mount the stairs, or grapple with a monstera in order to place a coffee cup on the sideboard, but a few well-chosen plants will transform a bare or dull room into something special in the same way as a carefully chosen picture or ornament.

Plants can also serve a functional purpose when used to screen off part of a room in a natural and much less obtrusive way than furniture or normal room dividers.

Establishing a style
Decide on the image and style that you intend to create, then buy plants that will help you to achieve it. Be prepared to invest in one or two really good specimens if necessary: they may cost no more than half a dozen mediocre plants yet will have far more impact. To create an old-fashioned cottage atmosphere, however, a collection of traditional plants on the win-

dowsill and a large aspidistra or sansevieria in an attractive cache-pot a more likely to achieve the right aml ence than some big, bold 'architect ral' plants that would create a stro statement in a large modern roo office, or foyer.

Groups or single specimens?
Most plants prefer to grow in grou as they benefit from the microclima produced, and three or five qu ordinary houseplants grouped in large container will make a far grea impact than they would if dott around the room individually. Grou ing plants usually means you have use a large container rather than ordi ary plant pots, and this also adds the sense of purpose and design.

Large plants can usually be used isolation, and many of the ta

ABOVE AND LEFT: *A good way to learn abo the best ways to arrange plants in the home to place the same plants in different containers or groups to see the very different effects you can create with the same plants. Here three cyclamen have been placed in separate containers (above) then grouped together in a single cache-pot (left). Both displays look elegant, but strikingly different.*

owers, such as yuccas, philo-
ndrons, and ficus such as *F. benjami-*
and *F. lyrata*, often have enough
sence to stand alone as focal point.
they become rather tall and bare at
base, however, you could try
nting some flowering plants, or
n small trailing ivies, in the same
ntainer to hide the stem.

ckgrounds and backdrops
st plants are best viewed against a
in background. If you have a highly
terned wall covering, especially if
ncludes leaves or floral motifs, the
nts you choose need to have big,
d foliage. This is where plain green
a definite advantage over varie-
ed foliage: visual chaos will result
m a boldly coloured and variegated
nt placed against a brightly deco-
ed wall covering.

king the most of height
all your plants are on tables or
ndowsills, they will look attractive
t predictable. Use a few large speci-
ns on the floor, or consider hanging
tainers in light corners of the room
t seem devoid of decoration at a
her level. Use trailers from the

Top: *Plants usually make a bolder feature
if grouped, and they benefit from the
microclimate produced. Here, the plants
have been graded in height to provide an
attractive foliage screen between the eating
and working areas of the kitchen.*

Above: *A disused fireplace can become a
focal point if used to frame plants. Use taller
plants in the hearth and smaller plants and
trailers on the mantelpiece.*

mantelpiece if you do not use the
fireplace, and make the most of pedestals for attractive containers with trailers like *Scindapsus aureus*, spiky upright plants like dracaenas or arching
plants like nephrolepsis ferns.

Choosing containers
Containers should never dominate,
but they can make a mediocre plant
look special, and many are ornaments
in their own right. Try using an
attractive ornament as a cache-pot for a
'plant, or if you have an interesting
container, like an old kettle or coalscuttle, plant it up with a flowering or
foliage plant that makes a happy mar-
riage and which does not dominate the
container.

A question of scale
The relationship between the size of
the plant and its required function in
the room should not be overlooked. A
solitary saintpaulia, even if it is set on
an attractive table, will make no impact in the overall composition; like-
wise, a large *Ficus benjamina* in a tiny
room in a cottage will certainly be
noticed, but not for its contribution
to the interior design.

Table-top displays

A BEAUTIFUL FLOWERING PLANT OR AN ARRANGEMENT OF FOLIAGE PLANTS
MAKES A SUPERB CENTREPIECE FOR A TABLE, WHETHER YOU USE IT AS A
FOCAL POINT ON A BARE TABLE OR AS THE CROWNING GLORY TO A
TABLE-SETTING FOR A DINNER PARTY. UNFORTUNATELY SUCH POSITIONS
SUIT FEW PLANTS, MOST OF WHICH PREFER A LIGHTER SPOT NEAR THE
WINDOW, SO CHOOSE YOUR PLANTS CAREFULLY AND BE PREPARED TO
CHANGE THEM FREQUENTLY.

Flowering plants

Give your table display a designer look
by choosing a flowering plant that is
colour co-ordinated with the tablecloth. This can look particularly pleasing if you are using the plant as part of
a table-setting for a meal, and even a
small plant will look effective if it
appears to have been chosen and displayed with care.

A cloth can be used to good effect
on a table used purely for display,
especially if the table itself is
mediocre. By choosing a patterned or
plain cloth that is light in colour, you
can draw attention to the feature, and
make even more of a focal point with
your plant. A cyclamen may look nice
but uninspiring if placed on a bare
table. But if you put it on a pink
tablecloth to match the shade of the
flower, it becomes something special.

Try positioning a bright flowering
plant with blooms on long stems, such
as a gerbera, on a side table with a
mirror behind. It will reflect the tall
blooms and appear to multiply the
number of flowers.

Gerberas are good examples of
flowering pot plants that are suitable
for a table display. They are usually
sold in bloom and are difficult to keep
for more than one year, so you might
treat them like a long-lasting display
of cut flowers. It will not matter that

the light is poor if the plant is to be
discarded after flowering, which
should continue for weeks.

Other flowering pot plants that will
bring colour and cheer to a dull corner
and that are usually discarded after
flowering include year-round chrysanthemums, cinerarias, *Erica × hyemalis*
and *E. gracilis*, and small annuals like
Exacum affine. In winter and spring,
bowls of bulbs such as hyacinths can
be used if you keep them in good light
until they come into flower and do not
try to force them to flower indoors the
following year.

Foliage plants

It is among the foliage plants that the
most shade-tolerant types are to be
found, but most are unsuitable for
table-tops. Most species of ficus, for
example, grow too large, while other
such as ivies, have a sprawling habit.
Choose something tough and
variegated, with a neat shape, such a
Sansevieria trifasciata gigantea 'Laure
tii', or variegated aglaonemas.

For a cool position, such as a
unheated bedroom, or a hall that
not too stuffy, varieties of *Aucu
japonica* are useful.

POT-ET-FLEUR

A *pot-et-fleur* arrangement makes an ideal centre piece, giving plenty of scope for artistic presentation. Anyone keen on floral art will find plenty of scope for expressing their talent.

To make a classic *pot-et-fleur* arrangement, choose an attractive planter (some self-watering pots are suitable), and plant a group of three to five foliage plants (you can plant more but the container needs to be large). As you plant them, insert a glass tube or metal florist's tube into the compost (potting soil), either at the centre of the arrangement or a little to one side.

Fill the tube with water and insert a few cut flowers (and cut foliage if you want). You won't need many flowers, yet they will bring a touch of colour to the arrangement, and because you have to replace them regularly the composition will be constantly changing. If one or two of the foliage plants begin to deteriorate in time, just replace them with fresh ones.

OPPOSITE ABOVE: *Colour co-ordinate your plants for a really tasteful effect. Here a pink cyclamen harmonizes with the tablecloth and wallpaper border.*

OPPOSITE LEFT: *Try placing a plant, like this gerbera, in front of a mirror where the reflection can make even a small plant look bigger and more imposing.*

RIGHT: *This* pot-et-fleur *arrangement uses floral foam to hold the cut flowers, which makes it particularly flexible in the way you can arrange the blooms. Lilies, freesias, cut ivy leaves and ivies were used to create the arrangement, here displayed in a hearth.*

Creating a pot-et-fleur with foam

1. If using a basket like this, line it first to ensure that it is waterproof.

2. Position your foliage plants first, preferably in shallow pots.

3. Cut floral foam to size to pack between the pots.

4. Insert your flowers (and additional cut foliage if wished) into the moist floral foam.

Pedestals and hanging pots and baskets

HANGING AND CASCADING PLANTS ARE ESPECIALLY USEFUL IF YOU WANT TO

MAKE THE MOST OF A VERTICAL SPACE OR CREATE A FEELING OF LUSHNESS IN

A GARDEN ROOM. WHERE SPACE IS LIMITED AND THE FLOOR ALREADY HAS

ITS BURDEN OF PLANTS, HANGING CONTAINERS CAN MAKE THE MOST OF THE

AVAILABLE SPACE. USE THEM TO CREATE CASCADING CURTAINS OF FOLIAGE.

Pedestals

Many pedestals are extremely orna
and make focal points in themselves
you have an attractive pedestal, do
cover it with long trailers that mask
beauty. Use short trailers that w
cascade over the pot but won't co
pletely hide the pedestal under a c
tain of leaves. Good plants to cho
for this effect include *Asparagus den.
lorus* 'Sprengeri', *Campanula isophy*
and flowering hybrids of zygocac
and rhipsalidopsis.

Plants with an arching rather tha
cascading habit are also ideal fo
pedestal where you want to show
both pot and pedestal: chlorophytu

ABOVE: *Chlorophytums look good displaye
on a pedestal or in a hanging basket, wher
the arching effect can be seen to advantage.
Hanging baskets are much more successful
a conservatory than indoors.*

LEFT: *The nephrolepis fern is a popular
choice for a pedestal, as it makes a neat
mound of growth with enough 'droop' to ta
the eye down to the pedestal. Here an
attractive table has been used, and the
opportunity taken to place another fern on
the shelf beneath.*

OPPOSITE LEFT: *Hanging baskets should
always be placed in a bright position, as t
light near the ceiling is almost always poo
than lower down the window. This one
contains a rhoicissus.*

d nephrolepis ferns are especially :ractive used in this way.

For a pedestal that is functional :her than decorative, go for tumb-ag curtains of growth, with plants :e ivies, *Plectranthus oertendahlii* and *coleoides* 'Marginatus', or a golden *ipremnum aureum* 'Neon' (syn. *Scin-osus aureus*).

anging pots and baskets

dinary hanging baskets are unsuit-le for using indoors, although you a of course use them in a conserva-ty. Unless you are prepared to take :at care with the watering, and take :cautions to avoid drips over your

carpets and furniture, choose a hang-ing pot with a drip tray, or a specially designed indoor 'basket' (in effect a basket-shaped pot, sometimes with a water reservoir).

Hanging containers are difficult to position: they shouldn't be hung where they can be a hazard to anyone walking by, and in addition many plants suitable for baskets need to be near good light. If the room is not large enough for hanging baskets, try the same plants in half baskets or wall pots. Many trailing or arching plants look magnificent when positioned against the background of a plain or pale wall.

PRACTICAL POINTS

 Pedestals are far more practical than hanging pots. The plants will usually be in better light (because sunlight generally shines downwards, the upper part of the room is generally gloomier than the lower part), and watering is much easier if the plants are grown in ordinary pots. Baskets are difficult to water, and need to be hung where the baskets and their trailing contents do not cause an obstruction to anyone walking by.

Planting a pedestal arrangement

1. A wide, shallow container, which is more stable and detracts less from the pedestal itself, has been chosen here.

2. Choose a mixture of flowering and foliage plants for a spectacular display. You can try them for position while still in their pots, until you are happy with the arrangement.

TRAILERS AND CASCADERS TO TRY

Flowering plants

 ieschynanthus, *Aporocactus* *agelliformis*, *Campanula isophylla*, olumnea, *Rhipsalidopsis gaertneri* and *ygocactus truncatus*.

 Foliage plants

 sparagus densiflorus 'Sprengeri', 'hlorophytum comosum 'Variegatum', *ipremnum aureum* (syn. *Scindapsus* ureus), *Hedera helix* (ivies), small-:aved varieties, plectranthus and hoicissus rhomboidea (syn. *Cissus* hombifolia).

3. Remove them from their pots for final planting. Try setting those at the edge at a slight angle so that they tend to grow outwards and tumble over the side.

RIGHT: *Don't just think of single specimens when choosing plants for a pedestal. A group can be arranged rather like a hanging basket, but planted in a pot.*

Grouping large plants

SOMETIMES A LARGE PLANT IS BEST VIEWED IN ISOLATION: ITS VERY SIZE AND IMPORTANCE WILL THEN BE EMPHASIZED. MORE OFTEN, HOWEVER, THEY LOOK BETTER WHEN POSITIONED AS PART OF A GROUP, PERHAPS WITH SMALLER PLANTS IN FRONT.

Group plants together in pla that might otherwise look bare. disused fireplace can be improv with perhaps a single, elegant fe provided that it is large enough. T whole fireplace and hearth area can the ideal place for a group of plant tall ones positioned mantelpie height at the back, smaller ones front at the bottom of the hearth, a arching or trailing plants sitting the mantelpiece.

If you have a really magnificent plant, perhaps a yucca 1.8m (6ft) tall or more, or a beautiful variegated *Ficus benjamina* that almost reaches the ceiling, show it off in splendid isolation. These plants deserve to act as focal points in their own right. Less imposing plants usually look better arranged in small groups, where they will make a greater impact than they would individually. You can create the effect of a garden brought indoors by positioning plants in this way. Plants standing shoulder to shoulder always look more convincing than those dotted around the room wherever there seems to be space to put a plant.

Small plants are easily grouped in a large planter, but this is not suitable for large specimens. The huge planters used in offices and hotel foyers are not practical for the home, and the plants are best left in their own pots and arranged in close proximity with the largest at the back and smaller ones in front.

The majority of large houseplants are grown for their foliage, but many are variegated or boldly coloured. It's a good idea to mix a few plants with coloured or variegated foliage among the greens, although you may sometimes need an all-green group to produce a cool, tranquil effect. Variegated plants also require higher light levels than all-green ones because a smaller area of the leaf is able to photosynthesize with what light is available, so it's best to avoid these for plant groupings in the darkest parts of the home.

Group policy

The natural way to group large house-plants is with the tallest at the back, with bushier, lower ones at the front. Take into account their position in the room. If the group is placed halfway down a long room with windows at each end, so that the plants act almost as a divider, include more plants in the arrangement, with smaller ones at each side and the tallest in the centre. In a corner of a room, a group of plants consisting of a single big specimen at the back, with smaller ones spilling forwards to fill out the corner, can look quite stunning.

If the plants in your group lack sufficient variation in height, try standing some on a low table or raise them in some other way.

To protect the floor, stand each pot in a saucer – those designed to match the pot look good and are perfectly practical. It is difficult to water plants at the back of a group, so the risk of a little water overflowing will be that much greater.

COMPATIBLE NEEDS

Wherever practical, group together those plants with similar needs. Yuccas and palms will tolerate a dry atmosphere and will be happy together, but most philodendrons and dracaenas prefer a humid atmosphere. For the short term you can mix any plants together, but if you plan to keep them in good condition, it's worth grouping plants with similar requirements so that they receive the most appropriate care.

OPPOSITE: *Plants often look better in groups, but choose ones appropriate to the setting. A group of small plants would look out of proportion in this hearth. The large specimens used here fill the space and give the setting a sense of design.*

TOP: *If this nephrolepis fern on a pedestal had been displayed on its own, it would probably have looked too isolated. By using it with other plants it looks interesting yet integrated.*

ABOVE: *Add one or two flowering plants to a group. Even a little colour will draw the eye.*

ABOVE: *Tall plants are always impressive, but they can look bare towards the base. By surrounding them with smaller bold plants in front, you can create a well planned group. A selection of all-green and variegated plants with a wide array of leaf size and shape have been selected here for maximum visual interest.*

Grouping small plants

SMALL PLANTS CAN BE DISPLAYED MORE CREATIVELY THAN JUST IN INDI-

VIDUAL POTS. PLANT THEM IN GROUPS IN PLANTERS OR SELF-WATERING

POTS. YOU CAN EVEN CREATE MINIATURE GARDENS.

Grouping plants together often makes them easier to care for, and they usually look more attractive as an arrangement rather than as individual plants.

The overall effect of a group is usually bolder than that of individual specimens, and by placing taller ones at the back of the arrangement the effect is more 'landscaped'. Small-leaved prostrate plants such as *Ficus pumila* and *Helxine soleirolii* (syn. *Soleirolia soleirolii*) assume a new role in a group and are less insignificant than when they are grown as prostrate plants in an individual pot. In a group they become ground-cover plants, which is their natural state. Another

advantage of grouping plants is th you can get away with less than pe fect specimens: a plant with lop-sid growth, or one that is bare at t base, can be arranged so that its d fects are hidden by other plants.

Grouped plants benefit from t microclimate created when plants a grown together. The local humidity likely to be a little higher as the leav tend to protect each other from dryi air and cold draughts, and it is eas to keep the compost (potting so evenly moist in a large container th a small one. Groupings are ideal f self-watering containers and for plar grown hydroponically, and simply e suring a steady and even supply moisture almost always produces be ter growth.

Grouping plants in a planter

1. A bowl without drainage holes will protect the table, but place a drainage layer at the bottom and be *very* careful not to overwater.

2. Place a little compost (potting soil) in the bowl first, then insert the plants. Try to achieve a good balance between flowering and foliage plants.

3. Firm the plants in, and pack more compost around the roots if necessary. Water, but be careful not to waterlog the compost.

ABOVE: *Pot up several plants in a bowl to make an attractive group; a* Begonia rex, *a cyclamen and ivies were used here.*

Group styles

There are no hard and fast rules abo how to group plants — whatev pleases you is right provided that t plants are also happy (avoid placi together plants with totally differe needs). The suggestions for groupi styles described here work well f most plants, and generally look attra tive, but be prepared to experiment. group of plants arranged in an c coalscuttle in the hearth, for examp may look more attractive than any the more traditional styles if the se ting is right.

Collections of pots have t advantage of being infinitely flexibl You can rearrange and remove plar at will, and use transient floweri plants such as chrysanthemums a poinsettias more easily than in permanent planting. A group of fi or six plants in their individual p will look cheery and bold if you m different types of foliage plants (st and upright, arching, feathery trailing) with a couple of floweri plants. You can space them out necessary to fill the space, but ma sure that they are close enough overlap a little and look like a grou

Pebble trays are ideal for plar that like a lot of humidity. Use a tr

at will fit on a table or windowsill,
d fill it with pebbles. Stand the
ts on the pebbles. It does not mat-
r if water stands in the tray provided
at the bottoms of the pots are not in
rect contact with it.

Planters and self-watering pots
ll usually accommodate at least
ree plants if you choose a suitable
e. These look elegant, and are ideal
you find regular watering difficult.
oose plants that will not need fre-
ent repotting or removing, and
ant directly into the compost (pot-
g soil).

WATCH OUT FOR PROBLEMS

Growing plants in groups has
ome drawbacks. Pests and diseases
an spread more easily and rapidly,
nd you may be less likely to notice
he early symptoms on leaves that are
idden by other plants. If grooming
s a regular routine, however, this
hould be only a minor drawback,
nd one that is easily overcome.

OVE: *Grouping small plants is*
ticularly effective if you need to use them
low position, where they are viewed from
e. Add some flowering plants (here
eras and begonias) to bring a foliage
p to life.

TOP: *Small plants benefit from grouping as*
much as large ones. You can often group
small plants in one large container, but by
keeping them in individual containers you
can ring the changes more easily. This is
especially important if you use flowering
plants that may look attractive for only a
relatively short time.

ABOVE: *Grouping plants in a shallow dish*
keeps them happy and looks good too. Because
these plants are raised on expanded clay
granules (you could use small gravel), some
water can be kept in the bottom without
waterlogging the compost (potting soil) –
providing invaluable humidity for the ferns.

Garden rooms and conservatories

WITH A GARDEN ROOM OR CONSERVATORY YOU CAN GROW ALMOST ANY HOUSEPLANT SUCCESSFULLY, AS WELL AS MANY MORE FOR WHICH YOU WOULD NORMALLY NEED A GREENHOUSE. HOWEVER, YOU WILL HAVE TO RESOLVE THE CONFLICT BETWEEN THE NEEDS OF PLANTS AND HUMANS, FOR WHAT IS A COMFORTABLE ENVIRONMENT FOR TROPICAL PLANTS MAY NOT BE COMFORTABLE FOR YOU. WITH CAREFUL PLANNING, HOWEVER, YOU CAN MAKE THE GARDEN ROOM AN EXTENSION OF THE LIVING AREA, WHERE YOU CAN ENJOY HOUSEPLANTS AT THEIR VERY BEST.

Many conservatories and garden rooms are built on as a home extension or a sun room where the garden can be enjoyed when the weather is pleasant but not warm, and in which the plants are merely decorative accessories. You can, however, create a veritable jungle atmosphere, with plants from floor to roof, and hot and humid air to match.

Mainly for people

If a sun room or conservatory is to be a comfortable place to sit for long periods and enjoy the view of the garden, a few attractive chairs, a coffee table and a few elegant pot plants dotted around are all that's required. It just becomes another room.

Paint the back wall white or cream, plant a bougainvillea against it, buy a few big palms and add one or two flowering shrubs such as *Nerium oleander*, and perhaps an orange or lemon in an attractive tub, and you will have a room with instant charm.

Mainly for plants

If your conservatory was bought mainly to increase the number and type of houseplants that you can grow, treat it like a greenhouse. Indeed the distinction between some modern lean-to greenhouses and garden rooms can be a little blurred.

Make the most of climbers; these will clothe the wall and cover the roof space if you secure galvanized wires at about 30–60cm (1–2ft) intervals for support. The roof cover will provide welcome shade in the summer, and if

you choose deciduous climbers such a grapevine or a passiflora, the oth inhabitants will receive full light the time of year when they most ne it. Even so, climbers such as grap may still need to be cut back periodically during the summer to preve them from dominating and casting t much shade.

Plant climbers and wall shrubs the ground if possible, by lifting t paving and making planting pits. U special display shelves, or improv your own. Don't just arrange plar around the edge of the structure, cr ate islands of plants, or use them a backdrop for seats, which can almost surrounded with plants.

Hanging baskets should thrive, use plenty of them and be adventur with what you plant. Although tra tional bedding plants can be used ir conservatory, cascading fuchsias curtains of columneas are usua much more spectacular.

For healthy houseplants, lay a flc that won't come to harm if you spla water about. Use a humidifier if po ible, so that the air is aways moist warm weather, and provide heating the winter. A minimum of 7°C (45° is sufficient to keep most housepla alive, while the majority of tend types will survive the winter at 13 (55°F) minimum.

OVE: *Bold, tall plants, like this palm,* *be used as an eye-catching feature in a* *servatory. It also emphasizes the vertical* *e of the magnificent wrought-iron* *rcase.*

POSITE: *Citrus fruits, such as oranges, do* *do well indoors, but they make excellent* *servatory plants. Try painting your* *servatory wall white to reflect light and to* *ke an attractive backdrop against which* *iew your plants.*

TOP RIGHT: *By keeping most of the planting* *around the edge, and using plenty of hanging* *baskets, you can give the impression of lush* *plant growth while still retaining an* *attractive sitting area.*

ABOVE RIGHT: *Make the most of available* *space. Plant climbers against the house wall,* *and use hanging baskets, which will do much* *better in the improved light than indoors.*

RIGHT: *Plants should thrive in a* *conservatory, and you can use bold all-green* *foliage groups like this. With a tiled floor* *you can provide plenty of moisture and* *humidity without worrying about drips or* *splashed water.*

Bottle gardens

BOTTLE GARDENS, CREATED IN SEALED BOTTLES WITH MOISTURE RECIRCU-

LATING AS IT CONDENSES AND RUNS DOWN THE GLASS, MAKE AN IDEAL HOME

FOR MANY SMALL BUT DEMANDING PLANTS THAT ARE DIFFICULT TO KEEP IN

A NORMAL ROOM ENVIRONMENT. THEY ALSO MAKE A VERY DECORATIVE WAY

OF DISPLAYING PLANTS AND ONE THAT IS SURE TO BECOME A TALKING POINT

WITH VISITORS.

The still, protected and humid e[n]vironment of a sealed bottle ga[r]den makes it possible to grow ma[ny] small jungle and rain forest type plan[ts] that would soon die in a dry livin[g] room. Yet if you leave the top off an[d] water very carefully, a bottle gard[en] can also be a pretty way to displ[ay] those that enjoy less humid cond[i]tions. Even flowering plants can [be] used if you are careful to deadhe[ad] them regularly to prevent the rotti[ng] flowers becoming a source of disease[.]

Sealed bottles will thrive for mon[ths] without attention, and you can go [on]

How to plant a bottle garden

1. Place a layer of charcoal and gravel or expanded clay granules in the bottom of a thoroughly clean bottle, then add compost (potting soil). Use a funnel or cone made from thick paper or thin cardboard as a guide.

2. Use small plants, and if necessary remove some of the compost to make insertion easier. Unless the neck is very narrow you should be able to insert the plants without difficulty.

3. After tamping the compost around the roots (use a cotton reel on the end of a can[e] if necessary), mist the plants and compost. necessary, direct the spray to remove compost adhering to the sides.

LEFT: *An open-topped bottle like this will require regular careful watering, but as it contains some quick growing plants the rea[dy] access makes routine grooming and pruning much easier.*

holiday confident that even tricky ferns and selaginellas will be safe until you return. Unsealed containers require careful watering, and if you use flowering or fast-growing plants in them, regular grooming and pruning are essential.

Bottle gardens can be difficult to display. The plants need good light, and if you choose a bottle with coloured glass (many of those readily available are green) it is important to remember that much of the useful light will be filtered out. A sunny window is as undesirable as a gloomy

corner: temperatures can soar as the sun's rays penetrate two layers of glass. The best place is by a window that does not receive direct sunlight, or on a table just below a sunny window, where it will receive good light but little direct sun.

Metal display stands make more of a feature of a bottle that would otherwise be placed on the floor, and help by raising it a little towards the light.

Sealed or open?

If you have a container with a stopper, a sealed environment will mean that

you can leave it for months without watering, *once the atmosphere has been balanced*. But these are not suitable for plants with flowers, or fast-growing foliage plants. Any plant used in a sealed bottle must be able to tolerate constantly damp, humid conditions, and poor light.

Tip

If you can't get your hand into the bottle, use a spoon tied to a cane to make the planting hole, and a fork tied to another one to hold the plant while you lower it into position.

BALANCING A SEALED BOTTLE

🌿 If you add too much water to a sealed bottle, the plants may rot and condensation on the glass will be a constant problem. If you add too little, the plants will not grow. You can only achieve the correct balance by trial and error.

🌿 If the compost (potting soil) looks or feels too wet, leave the stopper off for a few days until it begins to dry out.

🌿 It is normal for the bottle to mist up inside when the outside temperature drops, so a 'steamed up' bottle in the morning is not abnormal. If the condensation does not clear during the morning, the compost is too moist (leave the stopper off for a day). If there is no condensation when the room temperature drops significantly, the compost may be too dry.

ABOVE LEFT: *A large kitchen jar makes an interesting bottle garden. This one contains a miniature saintpaulia. Open the jar regularly to remove dead flowers, which will otherwise start to decay and cause the other plants to rot.*

FAR LEFT AND LEFT: *Bottle gardens can be used to display a variety of foliage plants, such as selaginella, variegated ivy and a colourful dracaena (far left). A collection of just one kind of plant, such as three different pileas (left), can also make an interesting group.*

Terrariums and other plant cases

TERRARIUMS AND PLANT CASES ARE USUALLY USED AS A DECORATIVE ORNA-
MENT, PERHAPS ON A SIDE TABLE WITH ADEQUATE ARTIFICIAL LIGHTING TO
SHOW OFF THE CONTAINER AND TO STIMULATE PLANT GROWTH, OR ON A
TABLE IN FRONT OF A WINDOW. KEEP THE PLANTS SIMPLE AND UNCLUT-
TERED IF YOU WANT TO MAKE THE MOST OF AN ATTRACTIVE CONTAINER;
CONCENTRATE ON A LUSH PLANTING IF THE CASE IS PRACTICAL RATHER
THAN PLEASING.

Terrariums and plants cases encom-
pass those containers that are not
bottles, but the advantages and chal-
lenges are exactly the same as for a
bottle garden. With a terrarium you
can let your imagination roam wider
in search of suitable containers. The
old-fashioned Wardian cases (now rare
and expensive, though replicas can be
found) are especially attractive, but a
second-hand aquarium will do just as
well and you may be able to obtain one
quite cheaply as it does not even have
to be watertight.

Some glass cases can be sealed, in
the same way as a bottle garden, but
most are left open. The plants are
protected from draughts on all sides,
and this helps to keep the atmosphere
warm and moist around the plants.

SUITABLE CONTAINERS

🦫 Elaborate terrariums are available
from garden centres and shops, but
you can sometimes buy kits to make
your own. Designs vary from plain to
ornate, but most are assembled with
glass cut to shape and held together
with strips of lead. Inexpensive,
improvised containers are often just
as successful if your interest lies in
the plants rather than in the
container.

🦫 **Aquariums** offer plenty of scope
for 'landscaping'. On the one hand
they can be used without a top and
kept fairly dry for a cactus garden,
complete with a suitably arid setting
of stones and stone chippings; on the
other they will make an ideal home
for delicate ferns if you create a
humid atmosphere by covering with
a glass top. You can buy aquarium
covers that include a light, enabling
you to make a feature of it even in a
dark corner. But be sure to use the
type of fluorescent tube sold for
aquariums, as these are balanced to
produce a quality of light that is
suitable for plant growth.

🦫 **Goldfish bowls** can be used for
just one or two plants. A single plant
like a saintpaulia will look good, or
choose a spreading small-leaved
carpeter such as *Helxine soleirolii*
(syn. *Soleirolia soleirolii*) that will
gradually creep up the sides and
then spill over the rim.

🦫 **Specimen jars**, originally used
to preserve biological specimens,
can be attractive, but they are more
difficult to obtain (try a laboratory
equipment supplier).

LEFT: *Miniature kalanchoes and miniature
saintpaulias can be depended on to provide
colour in any terrarium, but a contrasting
foliage plant, like the selaginella in this one
will improve the arrangement.*

Planting a terrarium

1. Always place a drainage layer at the bottom of the terrarium. Use gravel and charcoal or expanded clay granules to counter the effects of standing water.

2. Plants that are a little too tall for the terrarium, such as this palm, can be trimmed to size, but do not use fast-growing plants that would quickly dominate the smaller specimens.

3. If necessary, remove some of the compost (potting soil) from the root-ball and firm the plant in well.

Many containers used for terrariums have more room than bottles or preserving jars, so larger plants can be grown, and you don't have to worry so much if a vigorous member of the group tries to pop its head above the rim. Long or deep containers, such as an aquarium, also offer much more scope for 'landscaping', with small rocks, even miniature pools.

Follow the watering advice for bottle gardens and take care with preparation and planting:

- Place a layer of charcoal and gravel at least 1cm (½in) thick on the bottom.

- Use a sterilized potting or seed compost (medium), but avoid feeding or using a compost high in nutrients, otherwise the plants will soon outgrow their space.

- Add small rocks or pebbles if you want to 'landscape' the terrarium, but avoid wood as this may rot and encourage diseases.

- Cover the container with a sheet of close-fitting glass if appropriate, and if you want to create an enclosed environment.

ABOVE: *An attractive terrarium like this can be expensive to buy, but some people make their own, and you may be able to buy one in kit form to assemble yourself.*

RIGHT: *Saintpaulias are a good choice for a container with easy access for removing dead flowers. They benefit from the protected and humid atmosphere. Instead of planting them alone, use them with a carpet of moss or low-growing selaginellas.*

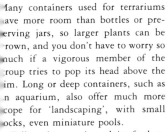

Specimen plants

EVERY HOME NEEDS AT LEAST A COUPLE OF SPECIMEN PLANTS TO PROVIDE ATTRACTIVE FOCAL POINTS. THEY DO NOT NEED TO BE LARGE SPECIMENS LIKE SMALL TREES, PROVIDED THAT THEY ARE IMPOSING. A WELL-ESTABLISHED CLIMBER THAT FORMS PART OF A ROOM DIVIDER, OR A REALLY LARGE ASPIDISTRA OR *NEPHROLEPIS EXALTATA* ON A PEDESTAL, FOR EXAMPLE, WILL SERVE THE SAME PURPOSE AS A LARGE *FICUS BENJAMINA* THAT ALMOST TOUCHES THE CEILING.

The purpose of a specimen plant is to catch the eye and be admired. This can be achieved by a really well-grown chlorophytum in a hanging container with cascading shoots carrying their small plantlets, as effectively as by an large, expensive palm. It just needs to be a superb example of the plant, well displayed, against a suitable background.

A large plant with a bold profile or outline, often called an 'architectural' plant, will transform a bare wall in a large room, add character to an otherwise uninspiring hallway, or give a sense of design and purpose if placed at the end of a long passage. If necessary, use spotlights to highlight the plant. If you use lights balanced for good plant growth the plant will benefit too. It is difficult to grow such large specimens yourself simply by starting with a small plant. It may take years and in the poor light and dry atmosphere indoors it will be extremely difficult to grow a plant to a large size without blemishes. Large specimens are expensive, however, so be sure that you can provide conditions that will maintain your investment.

Background and lighting
A bold plant requires a suitable background to show off its size and shape to advantage. A plain background is usually best, and a light-coloured wall will make most plants look good. If the background is colourful or confused, choose a plant with bold plain green leaves, such as a *Ficus lyrata*.

Once natural light fails, use spot lights to draw attention to key plants but make sure that the bulbs are no so close that the heat generated damages the plant.

Containers
Choose a container that does justice to the plant. An ordinary large plastic or clay pot will let down a magnificent palm or large weeping fig. If you want an ordinary terracotta pot, choose one that is large and ornately decorated (you don't have to worry about whether it is frostproof for indoors). I the décor demands something more modern, there are many very attractive planters and coloured plastic plant holders available.

Make sure that the colour of your chosen container goes with your décor and that the size is in proportion to the plant. A pot that is too large or too small will mar the effect.

OPPOSITE: *A single plant may be all that you need in a room if it's bold enough, like this majestic spathiphyllum.*

TOP LEFT: *You don't need to buy expensive or exotic plants for a specimen with real impact. The commonplace chlorophytum is so easy to grow and propagate that many plants are acquired as gifts from friends with surplus plants. If you keep a young plant for long enough, repot it annually, and are generous with the feeding and watering, you can end up with a magnificent specimen.*

ABOVE LEFT: Monstera deliciosa *is a firm favourite as a specimen plant, and this picture shows why. Here the clever use of a mirror not only makes the most of an attractive clock, but also reflects the bold leaves of the monstera.*

ABOVE RIGHT: *A large window or patio door with no sill needs a big floor-standing plant to create instant impact. Yuccas, and palms like this one, are ideal.*

PLANTS TO TRY

Architectural plants
Araucaria heterophylla (syn. *A. excelsa*), *Fatsia japonica*, *Ficus benjamina*, *Ficus elastica* varieties, *Ficus lyrata*, palms, *Philodendron bipinnatifidum* and yucca.

Climbing plants
Cissus antarctica, *Monstera deliciosa* and *Philodendron domesticum* (syn. *P. hastatum*).

Choosing a container

BESIDES FULFILLING AN ESSENTIAL FUNCTION, CONTAINERS CAN ALSO BE
DECORATIVE IN THEIR OWN RIGHT AND FORM PART OF THE ROOM DÉCOR
JUST LIKE A VASE OR ORNAMENT. THE RIGHT CONTAINER WILL ENHANCE AN
ATTRACTIVE PLANT AND CAN OFTEN COMPENSATE FOR A MEDIOCRE ONE.
THE CHOICE OF CONTAINER CAN DEMONSTRATE YOUR ARTISTIC FLAIR AND
EVEN YOUR SENSE OF HUMOUR.

Ordinary plant pots have a place in
the greenhouse, but not in the
home. Some plants, especially large
palms, benefit from the weight of a
large clay pot, which gives them stability if filled with a loam-based compost (potting soil), but indoors an
ornate one with an attractive pattern
will always look nicer than a plain one.
As a general rule, all other houseplants
look better in especially designed indoor containers.

Cache-pots

Repotting into a new container is not
always necessary. A cache-pot (an outer container in which you hide the pot
containing the plant) creates the right
illusion and avoids the need to repot.
This technique is especially useful for
flowering plants that will probably
only be in the home for a short time,
and for fast-growing plants that are
likely to need frequent repotting.

Any decorative container can be
used as a cache-pot. Attractive ones are
available in shops and garden centres,
but a search around the home often
provides something suitable. Even old
kitchenware, such as a teapot or copper saucepan, can look appropriate for
a plant in the kitchen.

If you are an amateur potter, making your own cache-pots can be particularly rewarding, and the plants provide a good opportunity to display
your talents around the home.

OPPOSITE ABOVE: *Sometimes a container that blends in with the background, like this fern-leaf basket, is as effective as one that contrasts with it.*

OPPOSITE BELOW: *If you don't have matching decorative containers for a group arrangement, improvise. Ordinary plastic pots and saucers have here been wrapped in strips of white cotton fabric for an eye-catching effect.*

ABOVE LEFT: *A metal container like this ornamental bucket adds to the crisp, clean look of a plant like* Asplenium nidus.

ABOVE CENTRE: *If you have a container with lots of character, like this antique 'self-watering' planter, choose a plant that does not detract from it. This* Asparagus plumosus *(syn.* A. setaceus*), has a feathery appearance that clothes the container without masking it.*

ABOVE RIGHT: *Containers like this decorative milk churn are great for kitchen herbs, such as parsley, but water very cautiously unless you can make drainage holes in the base.*

RIGHT: *This beautifully rounded container made from a hollowed-out pumpkin reflects the rounded shape and colour of the begonia it contains. As a finishing touch, moss has been draped around the plant and allowed to tumble over the rim of the container.*

Plastic and ceramic containers

A visit to any good garden centre will give you an idea of the huge choice of pretty yet practical containers that you can use. Whenever possible, choose one with drainage holes, otherwise you will have to treat it like a cache-pot or be *very* careful with watering. It is never a good idea to plant directly into any container without drainage holes. Even if you are careful about watering, sooner or later the roots will find themselves standing in water and, as a result of oxygen starvation, they will start to die.

Don't dismiss modern plastic containers. Some of them are bright, clean-looking and appropriate for a modern décor, or perhaps an office setting. Otherwise the choice of material and design must reflect your own taste and home décor.

Planters and self-watering containers

Planters are generally taken to mean containers that are large enough to hold several plants rather than individual specimens. These are ideal for displaying a group of plants.

Some planters are self-watering, with a reservoir at the bottom. Plants will generally thrive in these, and you can leave them for a few days with no problem. Although more expensive than ordinary containers, they are strongly recommended if plastic containers do not look incongruous in your home.

Think small as well as big

Very small plants are sometimes difficult to display, and a prostrate plant such as *Nertera depressa* can look slightly ridiculous grown in a normal pot — you will see more of the pot than of the plant. Try growing plants like these in small, decorative or fun containers, such as a collection of ducks or hens with a planting space in their backs. If you have a group of perhaps three such containers, planted with

WARNING WORDS

🪴 Cache-pots usually lack a drainage hole. This means that you don't have to bother with a saucer beneath the pot, but the plant inside will be standing in water and will soon die unless you are very careful about watering.

🪴 Place a few pebbles or marbles in the bottom, to raise the inner pot off the bottom of the container. If a little surplus water drains through, the compost (potting soil) should not remain soaked. But always check that the bottom of the inner pot is clear of any standing water.

🪴 If planting in any container without drainage holes, be *extremely careful* when watering. It's almost impossible to know whether there is standing water in the bottom of a container. You may want to risk it for a short-term plant that you know will have to be discarded soon, otherwise just use the container as a cache-pot or choose a different one.

TOP LEFT: *Glass containers can look very stylish. A lining of moss will look more attractive than exposed compost (potting soil). Careful watering is essential if you plant straight into any container without drainage holes.*

CENTRE LEFT: *Ornamental cabbages and kales are usually sold for outdoor decoration, but you can use them indoors for a few weeks. For a table-top display, try wrapping the plastic pot in a crisp white napkin.*

BELOW LEFT: *Sometimes the colour of a variegated leaf can pick up and extend the colour of the container. Here a variegated ivy tumbles out of a white teapot.*

BELOW RIGHT: *Low, mound-forming or carpeting plants such as* Helxine soleirolii *(syn.* Soleirolia soleirolii*) need a small container in proportion to the plant.*

OPPOSITE ABOVE: *Moss baskets make unusual containers for the right plants. This spathiphyllum looks right because the flower is taller than the handle.*

OPPOSITE BELOW: *Use a bit of lateral thinking in the kitchen. Try displaying some of your fruit with the flowers. Here oranges and apples share an interesting wooden container with* Streptocarpus saxorum.

matching or different prostrate plants, they will bring a touch of humour to your home, and should not seem to be in poor taste.

Baskets

Many foliage and flowering plants look especially attractive in wicker and moss-covered baskets, but if using a basket not specifically intended for plants, be sure to line it with a protective sheet. If you simply place pots into the basket, or replant into compost (potting soil) placed directly into the basket, moisture will seep through, mar any surface beneath, and in time rot or damage the basket.

Line the basket with a sheet of flexible plastic or any other waterproof membrane (a large piece of kitchen foil will do if you have nothing more suitable to hand). The protective liner can be taped down and should not be visible once the basket has been filled with compost and planted.

Small plants can look especially pretty in a basket with a handle, but taller plants can look awkward if the plant is very leafy or its height coincides with the top of the handle.

Search out the unusual

The container that is just right for a particular plant, or a special position, may be one that you will only recognize when you see it. Part of the fun of growing houseplants lies in using them creatively, and displaying them with imagination. Searching out fun or interesting containers can become part of the hobby.

Garden centres often have a useful range of containers to start with, but for the more stylish plant holders you may have to visit the kind of shop that sells well-designed furniture, stores that specialize in modern home accessories, and even antique shops. But you might find something just as good, and far less expensive, in a junk shop or even a jumble or garage sale. One person's throw-away may be a source of inspiration to a flower arranger or houseplant enthusiast.

Porch plants

USE YOUR PORCH TO GROW THE TOUGHER HOUSEPLANTS THAT NEED PLENTY

OF SPACE AND GOOD LIGHT. YOU CAN EVEN MAKE IT LOOK LIKE A SMALL

CONSERVATORY.

A porch influences the visitor's first impression of your home, so one that is well clothed with plants rather than bare and bleak will make a warmer welcome. An enclosed porch can be awash with colour the year round, but with an open porch in an exposed or cold position you will have to be content with hardy foliage plants for the cold months.

Enclosed porches

An enclosed porch can be like a mini lean-to greenhouse, and you can enjoy lush foliage and colourful flowers every month of the year. However, try to avoid using plants that will resent the sudden, icy blasts of air that occur when the outer door is opened in cold weather. Intolerant plants will soon drop their leaves and probably die.

Choose mainly plants recommended for cool temperatures, such as primulas, bowls of bulbs such as hyacinths and tulips, or cyclamen and azaleas for the winter. During the summer, regal and zonal geraniums (pelargoniums) do well in the hot atmosphere of such a small enclosed space, and cacti and succulents usually thrive. Provided that the porch can be maintained above freezing temperature, most cacti and succulents will benefit from being left there during the winter. The majority of cacti flower better if they have experienced a cold period during the winter.

Make use of climbers against at least one of the walls: passifloras would do well, but are generally too rampant. Choose something that is more easily restrained, such as *Hoya carnosa* or *Jasminum polyanthum* (be prepared to

ABOVE: *Porches can be bright or gloomy, protected or exposed. Choose plants appropriate to the conditions. This large* Ficus benajamina *will be happy in this position for the summer months, but will have to be brought indoors once the weather turns cold.*

keep it cut back once well established), or even a bougainvillea. Or go for foliage effect with *Cissus antarctica* or *Rhoicissus rhomboidea* (syn. *Cissus rhombifolia*).

If the porch is large, you can use plenty of big plants in floor-standing pots, such as *Fatsia japonica* (a variegated variety will look brighter in a porch), or perhaps an oleander (*Nerium oleander*).

Shelves will be needed to displa small plants. If there are no built-i shelves, use the small free-standin display units sold for greenhouses, o special plant stands.

Open porches

Even an open porch can be mad attractive. Group plenty of pots c hardy evergreens such as *Aucuba japc nica* varieties, *Fatsia japonica*, skim mias (most have attractive berries i winter), and ivies if you want a traile or climber. If you have pot-grow camellias and rhododendrons, for ex ample, you can bring them into th porch for extra colour when they ar in bloom.

Erica × *hyemalis*, *E. gracilis*, *Sola num capsicastrum* and its hybrids, ever year-round chrysanthemums, will a provide colour for weeks or eve months before having to be discarded

During the summer, many of th tougher indoor plants can be placed i your porch. Yuccas will do well, an the variegated chlorophytums are reli able, but you can use plants as divers as the brightly coloured coleus an flowering bougainvilleas. Don't b afraid to add a few unusual hardy foliage plants, such as rhubarb, t create a talking point.

PRACTICAL PROBLEMS

🐾 Most houseplants will thrive in an enclosed porch if you avoid extremely high or low temperatures.

🐾 A small electric heater coupled to a thermostat will keep it frostproof at little cost, and a fan heater will warm the air rapidly when the door is open. But blasts of cold are hard to avoid, so don't persevere with plants that seem to resent the position.

🐾 Too much heat is the main problem in summer. Unlike a greenhouse or conservatory, ventilation is often inadequate. If the porch is in a position where it receives a lot of direct sun, be sure to fit at least one automatic ventilator and, whenever possible, open all the windows before the temperature rises. However, bear in mind that these solutions may affect the security of your property.

🐾 Shading will help, and you may find the shade offered by a climber more acceptable than blinds or shading paints.

OPPOSITE: *This large regal pelargonium is kept indoors as a houseplant, but moved to the porch in full flower so that it can be shared with passers-by.*

ABOVE: *This indoor yucca is happy to stand outdoors for the summer in a sheltered position, and it gives height and 'presence' to the rest of the group, which is made up of tough houseplants that will also tolerate cold conditions.*

RIGHT: *The porch is where indoor plants can rub shoulders with hardy plants. Here, a tender begonia has been used with hardy miniature daffodils grown in a pot, and a pot-grown rosemary. The miniature roses were bought as houseplants but will later be planted in the garden. The rhododendron is totally hardy.*

Living-rooms

THE LIVING-ROOM IS THE PLACE WHERE MOST PEOPLE GROW THEIR HOUSE-PLANTS. IT IS LIKELY TO BE WARM AND LIGHT, WITH PLENTY OF SPACE TO DISPLAY PLANTS CREATIVELY.

The living-room is probably the best room for houseplants. There are usually large windows – often ceiling to floor patio doors at one end – plenty of standing places such as windowsills, tables and ledges or alcoves, and usually ample space for large floor-standing specimens. It is also the room that most people make an effort to decorate attractively, and where they spend most of their leisure time.

Just as the appearance of a room can be changed by moving the furniture around, so the positioning of plants can radically alter how a room looks. This is especially true for large specimen plants that act as focal points, and for groups of large plants used to screen areas.

In living-rooms, the colour and texture of plants can play important roles, especially the way in which they blend or contrast with the background. Try to use the juxtaposition of contrasting forms, shapes and colours to emphasize the visual impact of the plants.

Colour always needs to be considered. A foliage or flower colour that blends with an accompanying pot o ornament will look tasteful, but th wall behind will look best if it i neutral, or plain and contrasting. Bu for a special effect you may want t blend the colours of your plants with more decorative background perhaps white daisy-like flowers wit green ferns, and green-and-whit dieffenbachia against white net curtains, all set off on a white table.

Texture adds variety. The lon purple hairs of a gynura will be bes emphasized by a smooth pale background, a prickly cactus may loo more in keeping with the colour an texture of rough bricks behind. Th papery, wing-like leaves of caladium will need a colour behind that bring out the beauty of these exotic-lookin leaves (as they vary from white an green to bright red, the best background depends on the variety). Bu above all, the leaves of caladiums nee to be illuminated well, either fro behind or in front, to show off the delicate texture. The puckered leave of the *Begonia masoniana* have a textur that you want to touch, adding tacti to visual stimulation.

Shape will compensate for lack colour. Most philodendrons hav large and interestingly shaped leave like the fingered and fringed *P. bipi natifidum* and the more deeply cut *F selloum*, and among the large-leave ficus, *F. lyrata* has enormous, wax leaves the shape of an upside-dow violin. Plants like this will create much interest as those with brigh flowers or brilliant foliage, and the do it in a restrained way that create the right mood for an elegant an sophisticated living-room.

Making a mini cactus garden

1. Make sure there are adequate drainage holes. Cover these with pieces of broken pot.

2. Although a cactus compost (potting soil) is preferable, you can use an ordinary compost.

3. If you have a very prickly cactus to plant, hold it in a strip of folded paper like this.

LEFT: *Cacti and succulents often look best i small groups, and a half-pot or shallow cl container is particularly appropriate.*

ABOVE: *Living rooms are usually light and spacious. Plants like aglaonemas, which like bright light but not direct sunlight, often do well by a window with net curtains. White net curtains make an excellent backdrop for many plants.*

RIGHT: *The living room is where you might want to use an especially beautiful container as a cache-pot for an appropriately impressive plant, like this azalea. As the blooms on one flowering plant die, replace with another, so that your special corner of the room always looks fresh and colourful.*

FAR RIGHT: *Succulents like this crassula are undemanding provided you can give them a position near the window. As they lack colour, try using a bright pot.*

Kitchens

IN THE DAYS WHEN KITCHENS WERE DARK AND DINGY AND COOKING WAS

DONE WITH COAL GAS, OR EVEN AN OPEN RANGE, THE KITCHEN WAS A PLACE

FOR ONLY THE TOUGHEST OF PLANTS. MODERN KITCHENS ARE USUALLY

LIGHT, BRIGHT AND RELATIVELY SPACIOUS. PLANTS SHOULD THRIVE HERE,

AND THERE ARE PLENTY OF OPPORTUNITIES TO USE THEM.

PROBLEM SPOTS

🐛 Bear in mind that heat rises, so do not place any plants where the heat from cooking will make life uncomfortable – on shelves or cupboards near the cooker for example.

🐛 Few houseplants will be happy with icy blasts from an open back door in winter. If possible, keep your plants well away from the door.

A s always, the windowsill is the first place to fill with plants. Here you can grow those that need good light, but if the room receives direct sun at the hottest part of the day you will be restricted to those that tolerate the sun's rays intensified by the glass, such as cacti and succulents, geraniums (pelargoniums) and tradescantias.

Make the most of the tops of cupboards near the window for trailing plants. Although watering can be difficult, and the light near the ceiling will be poor, as the plants trail and tumble they enter the zone of better light and most will thrive. If they become thin and straggly, keep pinching back the long shoots to keep the growth bushy and compact.

Avoid trailing or cascading plants on or near work surfaces or eating areas. Choose plants with upright growth that will not get in the way. *Sansevieria trifasciata* 'Laurentii', upright dracaenas, especially those on a mini trunk, clivias and aglaonemas are among the plants that look good and won't get in the way of normal kitchen activities.

Practical pot plants
Many cooks like the idea of having culinary herbs on hand to pluck straight from pot to pot. Unfortunately, if you use herbs a great deal in your cooking, your herb plants will not remain attractive for long! So don't

expect your indoor herbs to keep th kitchen supplied, but they will creat the right mood and aromas, and you can raid the plants for a leaf or two i an emergency. Nearly all herbs nee good light, and the best place for then is by a bright window.

You can place individual pots on th windowsill, but it is more effective and better for the plants, if you stand them all on a tray covering the lengt of the window and filled with grave on which to stand the pots. Some such as basil and pot marjoram, wi need turning regularly to even up th growth, and regular pinching out o the growing tips is essential for man herbs. Unless you pinch out the grow ing tip, and later subsequent mai shoots, basil will grow tall, flower an then deteriorate before you can harves much of a crop. Marjoram needs to b pinched back regularly to keep it com pact: the flowers are pretty, but a untamed plant will be too big an bushy for a windowsill.

Young plants of shrubs such as sag (*Salvia officinalis*) and rosemary (*Ro marinus officinalis*) are inexpensive t buy and are worth growing as youn pot plants. They will deteriorate in doors long before they become th large shrubs that you see in gardens but they will enhance the kitchen for season. If they are still alive and hea thy the following spring, plant ther in the garden, and buy another sma plant for indoors.

Planting a herb windowbox

1. For an inexpensive improvised windowbox, use a polystyrene (styrofoam) trough. You can paint it to suit the decor.

2. Always insert a layer of drainage material, such as gravel and charcoal or expanded clay granules, before filling with potting compost (medium).

3. Choose small, bushy plants wherever possible. Some will eventually grow too tall, but you can usually restrict the height by repeatedly pinching out the growing tips.

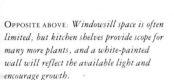

OPPOSITE ABOVE: Windowsill space is often limited, but kitchen shelves provide scope for many more plants, and a white-painted wall will reflect the available light and encourage growth.

OPPOSITE BELOW: Use trailers like this Philodendron scandens *where its cascading stems won't get in the way. Near working surfaces, choose compact plants like this variegated* Tolmiea menziesii.

CENTRE RIGHT: An indoor or outdoor windowbox full of herbs will not keep you supplied with all you need for culinary use, but it's a fun feature and may extend the season of fresh herbs when those outdoors are no longer available. This windowbox contains (from left to right) basil, thyme, parsley, rosemary and variegated apple mint.

BELOW RIGHT: The vacant space on top of cupboards can be used for low-growing or trailing plants, but bear in mind that light levels are often low, trailers may interfere with opening doors and watering can be difficult.

BELOW FAR RIGHT: Codiaeums usually do well in a kitchen provided you avoid a position exposed to cold draughts.

Bedrooms

IF YOUR ENTHUSIASM FOR PLANTS OUTGROWS THE SPACE AVAILABLE IN
TRADITIONAL DISPLAY AREAS SUCH AS THE LIVING-ROOM AND KITCHEN,
OVERCOME PREJUDICE AND MAKE YOUR BEDROOM MORE BEAUTIFUL, TOO.

Many people are deterred from placing plants in their bedroom on the grounds that they are 'unhealthy'. However, plants will not deprive you of oxygen, and the reluctance to use them in the bedroom is no more than prejudice. You will probably find it a more restful place with the added greenery of a few plants, and you can even wake up to the perfume of stephanotis or hyacinths.

Bedrooms are often kept cooler than living-rooms, and this is an advantage for many plants. Winter-flowering plants, in particular, often last much longer in a cool atmosphere.

Suitable plants
Plants in bedrooms are probably viewed less than those in other parts of the house. Although we spend many hours there, most of them will be spent asleep, which means the plants are sometimes neglected.

Bedrooms are an excellent place for a collection of cacti and succulents and for large individual specimens of tolerant foliage plants such as aspidistras and scindapsus (epipremnums) which are unlikely to become stressed if forgotten for a day or two.

If you can discipline yourself to water and mist them regularly, however, even delicate ferns will often do well because the air is usually more humid than in a hot living-room.

Fragrant plants can be especially pleasing, and the strongest scents will be appreciated beyond the bedroom itself if you leave the door open.

Bedside tables and dressing tables
Plants can add the finishing touch to a dressing table or a bedside table, but these are usually areas where natural light levels are low. Table lamps can display the plant to advantage after dark, but these do little for plant growth (and if too near, may scorch the plant). Be prepared to move your plants around, giving them a week or

two at most in these positions, then rotate them with other plants that have had a spell in better light.

A place for plants to rest

Although you will want your bedroom to look well-designed and furnished with pretty or attractive plants, you may want to use a spare bedroom as a resting place for all those plants that are so perfect for a short time but border on the unattractive for the rest of the year. 'Resting' orchids and ephiphyllums, and tender primulas that have finished flowering, for example, are among the candidates for a light position in a bedroom. You can move them into a prominent position when they come into bloom again.

OPPOSITE ABOVE: *Instead of using air fresheners, wake up to the fragrance of real flowers, provided by plants such as this* Stephanotis floribunda.

OPPOSITE BELOW: *Enjoy the delicate perfume of* Jasminum polyanthum *as you sit at your dressing table. Dressing-table plants should be used at their prime, then moved to a lighter and more appropriate position to recuperate.*

ABOVE RIGHT: *If you adore the heady scent of gardenias, try one on your bedside table. . When flowering has finished, move it to a lighter position.*

RIGHT: *Many bromeliads bought in bloom are discarded after flowering, so they can be used on a table well away from the window. This one is* Vriesea splendens, *with a distinctive flower spike that can be 60cm (2ft) long. The yellow* Celosia plumosa *is an inexpensive annual which can be used as a short-term houseplant for a few weeks.*

Halls and landings

HALLS AND LANDINGS PRESENT BOTH PROBLEMS AND OPPORTUNITIES. THE LIGHT IS OFTEN POOR, SPACE SOMETIMES CRAMPED AND COLD BLASTS FROM THE OPEN FRONT DOOR IN WINTER ALL PROVIDE UNPROMISING CONDITIONS FOR PLANTS. BUT THERE ARE STILL SOME THAT WILL THRIVE AND EVEN LOOK GOOD ENOUGH TO MAKE YOU LINGER TO ADMIRE THEM. IF YOU ARE A HOUSEPLANT ENTHUSIAST YOU'LL WANT TO MAKE THE MOST OF ALL THE GROWING SPACE AVAILABLE.

In some centrally heated homes, halls and stairways are as warm as any other part of the house, in others they are often cold and lack sufficient natural light. Despite these drawbacks one survey showed that more than a third of people who grow houseplants have at least some of them in the hall, and probably many more would if they could find plants that would thrive there. The plants suggested here are tough enough to grow even where these imperfect conditions exist, but in any place where there is enough winter warmth, conditions can be improved by using plenty of artificial light to make a feature of your plants.

It is always better to have one or two well-displayed, tough evergreens that look really lush and healthy, than to struggle with lots of colourful exotics that end up looking sickly.

Large plants
One or two specimen plants used as focal points will impress visitors on their arrival. Depending on the layout of your hallway, place one at the end of the passage leading to the door, in the vestibule where the doors opens, or on the landing or top of the stairs if there is space. Good plants for this purpose are large specimens of *Ficus benjamina* (a variegated variety is especially effective in this situation), *Monstera*

ABOVE: *Plants on stairs must always be used with caution, but where you have space, as with this turn in the stairs, a few plants will transform what would otherwise be a featureless part of the house.*

deliciosa, Dracaena deremensis, Schefflera actinophylla, Yucca elephantipes, or a tough palm such as *Howeia forsteriana* (syn. *Kentia forsteriana*). If the position is gloomy during the day, use fluorescent lights balanced for plant growth, or spotlights recommended for plants.

Make sure that your décor shows off specimen plants to their best advantage: a plain, light-coloured wall is particularly effective, and a mirror placed behind a plant will deflect the light, perhaps making the hall look larger, as well as reflecting the plant itself. A white or cream-coloured ceiling will also help to reflect light.

Climbers and trailers
Provided that using plants will never become a danger to anyone in this area, stairwells provide a great opportunity for luxuriant climbers and trailers to grow freely.

Troughs filled with trailers, placed on a balcony along the stairwell, will enable the plants to tumble over the edge to provide a living curtain. A climber in the hall or at the bottom of the stairs can sometimes be trained to grow along the banister.

Climbers that often thrive in hall conditions include *Rhoicissus rhomboidea* (syn. *Cissus rhombifolia*) and the small-leaved varieties of the ordinary ivy (varieties of *Hedera helix*).

You can let ivies trail too, but more interesting are *Philodendron scandens* and *Epipremnum aureum* 'Neon', both of which will produce long trails of growth. *Plectranthus australis* and *P. coleoides* 'Marginatus' are also vigorous trailers that will soon produce a hanging curtain of foliage.

Table plants
One of the most popular positions for a hall plant is on a small table near the front door. If the door and the surrounding area are solid you might find cut flowers more successful here, but if they are mainly glass, conditions will be ideal for a plant that does not object to cold draughts. Be warned, however, the patterned glass sometimes used in this situation can act like a magnifying glass and scorch leaves directly in the sun's rays.

Dependable plants for a hall table with reasonable light are chlorophytums, and two tough ferns: *Cyrtomium falcatum* and *Asplenium nidus*.

ABOVE: *If you have a hall with an old-fashioned look or an ambience associated with antiques, choose a large plant for the entrance, such as a palm, large ficus, or even a tall bamboo, but make sure it will cope with blasts of cold air in the winter.*

RIGHT: *If you use white or pale walls to reflect the light, some plants will do quite well even away from a window. Here a fern makes a statement of elegance in an area that could otherwise look bare.*

FAR RIGHT: *Floor-standing plants for landings must be chosen with care. Although height is useful, it is important that the plant does not cause an obstruction. Try to position the plant in a corner. The white walls of this landing help to reflect light and show the plant off to advantage.*

Bathrooms

BATHROOMS ARE NOT THE PARADISE FOR PLANTS THAT SOME PEOPLE THINK.

ALTHOUGH THE HUMIDITY IS OFTEN HIGH, THERE ARE DRAWBACKS TOO, SO

CHOOSE YOUR PLANTS WITH CARE.

The average bathroom has conditions that prevail nowhere else in the home: short periods of high temperature and high humidity contrasting with much longer spells of quite cool conditions (especially if the central heating is not kept on permanently), and because the windows are often small, poor natural light. The plants may also have to contend with the use of aerosols and sprays containing a variety of chemicals for personal care, and often a liberal dusting of talcum powder too. These are not conditions in which the majority of houseplants will thrive.

Good positions

Try to keep foliage out of reach of splashes from the bath and wash-basin. Pots perched on the edge or back of the bath are in a precarious position, and the chances are that the light will also be poor.

Make the most of the windowsill, especially for flowering plants. Further into the room, use tough foliage plants such as aspidistras and asparagus ferns, perhaps in front of a mirror, where they will receive reflected light and the mirror will make the plants look larger.

Tolerant trailers such as ivies and *Philodendron scandens* look good hanging from a high shelf, perhaps framing a mirror.

CARING FOR YOUR PLANTS

Bathroom plants need more regular grooming than those growing elsewhere. Leaf cleaning in particular should be done at least once a week. It is difficult to remove powder from plants with hairy leaves, so it is best to avoid these. If other plants become very coated with sprays or powder, try submerging the leaves briefly in water especially if there is so much foliage that it is tiring or impractical to wipe each leaf individually. If you splash soap, shampoo or toothpaste over a leaf, wipe it off immediately. If poor light is causing growth to arch towards the window, turn the plant regularly.

As soon as a plant appears to look unhappy, change it for another one. When the first one has recovered after a month or two in better conditions, rotate them again.

LEFT: *Plants may have to be concentrated near the window as bathrooms are not usually well illuminated with natural light, but by using plenty of plants on all available surfaces, the effect can be particularly pleasing.*

Use small flowering plants such as saintpaulias and kalanchoes on a make-up table or vanity unit, using attractive cache-pots that suit the setting. These will not make long-term bathroom plants, but they will look good for weeks before you have to move them on.

SUITABLE PLANTS

The following plants generally do well:

Large plants
Fatsia japonica, *Monstera deliciosa* and *Philodendron bipinnatifidum*.

Trailers
Epipremnum aureum (syn. *Scindapsus aureus*), *Philodendron scandens* and small-leaved ivies.

Bushy plants
Aglaonema species and varieties, *Aspidistra elatior* and *Chamaedorea elegans* (syn. *Neanthe bella*).

Short-term flowering plants
Chrysanthemum, cyclamen and exacum.

ABOVE RIGHT: *Plants as diverse as the hardy ivy and tricky* Asplenium capillus-veneris *an thrive in a bathroom. The ivy is good for ow light levels, and the fern will appreciate he frequent spells of high humidity.*

RIGHT: Philodendron scandens *is a good hoice for a trailer, while a spathiphyllum lways looks elegant with its glossy green eaves and white sail-like flowers. lowering plants, such as the cyclamen, can e brought in as short-term plants.*

AR RIGHT: *Use trailers with imagination. Bathrooms usually have small windows and end to be relatively gloomy, but by rotating he plants between rooms periodically you can eature attractive plant displays in all areas f the home.*

Glossary

Aerial root A root that grows from the stem above ground level. Plants such as philodendrons use them to assist climbing, as well as to absorb moisture and food.

Alkaline compost A growing medium containing lime, and having a high pH level.

Annual A plant that lives for only one year.

Bract A modified leaf, often vividly coloured and serving to attract pollinating insects to insignificant flowers that lack bright petals.

Bromeliad A member of the Bromeliaceae family. Most are ephiphytic, and the leaves usually form a rosette.

Bulb Although the term is often used to include corms and tubers, a bulb is strictly a structure consisting of modified leaves that protects the next season's embryo shoot and flowers.

Bulbil A small bulb that forms above ground on a few plants. Bulbils can be removed and potted up to grow into normal bulbs.

Callus A growth of corky tissue that forms over a wound, sealing and healing it.

Capillary mat An absorbent mat that holds a lot of water. Plants placed on it can draw up moisture by a capillary action.

Chlorophyll The green colouring pigment in plants, which enables them to manufacture food from sunlight (photosynthesize).

Chlorosis An unhealthy yellowing of the foliage, usually caused by a deficiency of iron or other trace elements.

Often appears in lime-hating plants which have been grown in an alkaline medium.

Compost (potting soil) The medium in which pot plants are grown.

Corm A swollen stem base that usually remains underground and stores food during the dormant season. If cut across, no distinct layers of leaves can be seen, unlike a bulb.

Crocks Pieces of broken clay pot (also known as shards), placed over the drainage hole of a clay pot to prevent the compost (potting soil) from being washed through the hole.

Crown The point at which stem and roots meet.

Dormant period The time when growth slows down and the plant needs less warmth and water. Some plants have no discernible dormant period, but with others – such as cyclamen – it is pronounced.

Epiphyte A plant that grows above ground level, usually in trees. Epiphytes are not parasites and only use their host for physical support.

Foliar feed A quick-acting liquid fertilizer that can be absorbed through the leaves as well as the roots.

Genus A group of species with enough common characteristics to group them together as a 'family'.

Hardy Frost-tolerant.

Hormone, rooting hormone An organic compound that stimulates a cutting into forming roots.

Humidifier A device for raising the humidity in a room. Simple ones are trays of water that work through evaporation, sophisticated ones are electrically powered.

Hydroponics A method of growing plants in nutrient solutions, without compost (potting soil).

Loam-based compost (potting soil) A soil mix in which the main ingredient is sterilized loam, to which peat (peat moss), sand and fertilizer are normally added.

Lux The scientific unit by which light levels are measured.

Offset A small plant that is produced alongside its parent.

Peat-based compost (peat-moss based potting soil) A soil mix in which peat is the main ingredient. Sometimes sand and other substances are added, and always fertilizers and something to neutralize the acidity of the peat. Peat substitutes, such as coir, are increasingly used to avoid depletion of natural peat reserves.

Perennial A plant that lives for more than two years.

Perlite An inert growing medium sometimes used as a compost (potting soil) additive or for rooting cuttings.

Petiole A leaf stalk.

pH A scale expressing the degree of acidity or alkalinity of a substance. It runs from 0 to 14, 7 being technically neutral, though most plants prefer a pH of about 6.5. Above 7 is alkaline below 7 is acid.

Photosynthesis The mechanism by which plants convert sunlight into energy.

Pot-bound A term used to describe a plant with roots that have filled the pot and are now beginning to inhibit growth.

Relative humidity The amount of water contained in the air at a particular temperature. It is calculated against the maximum amount of water that could be held in the air at that temperature.

Resting period (see **Dormant period**)

Rhizome A horizontal stem, on the surface or just below, and a form of storage organ.

Root-ball The mass of roots and compost (potting soil) together.

Sphagnum moss A moss belonging to the genus *Sphagnum*, found in boggy places and capable of holding a large amount of water.

Tuber A swollen underground stem or root. The plant's way of storing food during the dormant period.

Vermiculite An inert growing medium, sometimes used as a compost (potting soil) additive or for rooting cuttings.

Index of common plant names

African violet – Saintpaulia
Air plant – Tillandsia (some)
Aluminium plant – *Pilea cadierei*
Angel's trumpet – *Datura suaveolens* (syn.
  Brugmansia suaveolens)
Angel's wings – Caladium
Arabian violet – *Exacum affine*
Asparagus fern – *Asparagus densiflorus, A.
  plumosus* (syn. *A. setaceus*)
Autumn crocus – Colchicum
Baby's tears – *Soleirolia soleirolii* (syn. *Helxine
  soleirolii*)
Banyan tree – *Ficus benghalensis*
Barbeton daisy – Gerbera
Barrel cactus – *Echinocactus grusonii*
Bead plant – *Nertera depressa*
Begonia, fibrous-rooted – *Begonia semperflorens*
Bengal fig – *Ficus benghalensis*
Bird's nest fern – *Asplenium nidus*
Bird of paradise – *Strelitzia reginae*
Boston fern – *Nephrolepis exaltata* 'Bostoniensis'
Brake fern – *Pteris cretica*
Bush violet – Browallia
Busy Lizzie – Impatiens
Button fern – *Pellaea rotundifolia*
Canary date palm – *Phoenix canariensis*
Candle plant – *Plectranthus colcoides* 'Marginatus'
Cape primrose – Streptocarpus
Carpathian bellflower – *Campanula carpatica*
Cast iron plant – *Aspidistra elatior*
Chandelier plant – *Kalanchoe tubiflora* (syn.
  Bryophyllum tubiflorum)
Chinese evergreen – Aglaonema
Chinese hibiscus – *Hibiscus rosa-sinensis*
Christmas cactus – *Zygocactus truncatus* (syn.
  Schlumbergera truncata)
Christmas cherry – *Solanum capsicastrum, S.
  pseudocapsicum*
Cigar plant – *Cuphea ignea*
Cineraria – botanically *Senecio cruentus* (syn. *S.
  hybridus*)
Coconut palm – *Cocos nucifera*
Common wax plant – Hoya, *Stephanotis
  floribunda*
Creeping fig – *Ficus pumila*
Croton – Codiaeum
Crown cactus – Rebutia
Crown of thorns – *Euphorbia milii* (syn. *E.
  splendens*)
Curly palm – *Howeia belmoreana* (syn. *Kentia
  belmoreana*)
Desert fan palm – Washingtonia
Devil's backbone – *Kalanchoe daigremontiana*
  (syn. *Bryophyllum daigremontianum*)
Devil's ivy – *Scindapsus aureus* (syn. *Epipremnum
  aureum*)

Dragon tree – Dracaena
Dumb cane – Dieffenbachia
Easter cactus – *Rhipsalidopsis gaertneri* (syn.
  Schlumbergera gaertneri)
European fan palm – *Chamaerops humilis*
False castor oil plant – *Fatsia japonica*
Fiddle-leaf fig – *Ficus lyrata*
Flame nettle – Coleus
Flaming Katy – *Kalanchoe blossflediana*
Flaming sword – *Vriesea splendens*
Flamingo flower – Anthurium
Floss flower – Ageratum
Freckle face – *Hypoestes sanguinolenta* (syn. *H.
  phyllostachya*)
Geranium, scented-leaved – Pelargonium
Gloxinia – botanically *Sinningia speciosa*
Grape ivy – *Cissus rhombifolia* (syn. *Rhoicissus
  rhomboidea*)
Holly fern – *Cyrtomium falcatum* (syn. *Polystichum
  falcatum*)
Inch plant – Tradescantia and Zebrina
Iron cross begonia – *Begonia masoniana*
Italian bellflower – *Campanula isophylla*
Ivy – *Hedera helix*
Ivy tree – x *Fatshedera*
Japanese aralia – *Fatsia japonica*
Jasmine, white – *Jasminum officinale*
Jasmine, pink – *Jasminum polyanthum*
Jerusalem cherry – *Solanum capsicastrum, S.
  pseudocapsicum*
Joseph's coat – Codiaeum
Kangaroo vine – *Cissus antarctica*
Kentia palm – *Howeia forsteriana* (syn. *Kentia
  forsteriana*)
Lacy tree philodendron – *Philodendron selloum*
Ladder fern – Nephrolepis
Lady's slipper – Cypripedium (syn.
  Paphiopedilum)
Madagascar dragon tree – *Cordyline terminalis*
  (syn. *Dracaena terminalis*)
Maidenhair fern – Adiantum
Mexican breadfruit – *Monstera deliciosa*
Mind your own business – *Soleirolia soleirolii*
  (syn. *Helxine soleirolii*)
Mother fern – *Asplenium bulbiferum*
Mother of thousands – *Saxifraga stolonifera* (syn.
  S. sarmentosa)
Mother-in-law's tongue – *Sansevieria trifasciata*
  'Laurentii'
New Zealand cliffbrake – *Pellaea rotundifolia*
Norfolk Island pine – *Araucaria heterophylla* (syn.
  A. excelsa)
Oleander – *Nerium oleander*
Orchid cactus – Epiphyllum
Painted net leaf – *Fittonia verschaffeltii*
Pansy orchid – Miltonia
Paper flower – Bougainvillea

Parasol plant – *Schefflera arboricola* (syn.
  Heptapleurum arboricola)
Parlour palm – *Chamaedorea elegans* (syn. *Neanthe
  bella*)
Peace lily – Spathiphyllum
Pepper, annual – *Capsicum annuum*
Persian violet – *Exacum affine*
Piggyback plant – *Tolmiea menziesii*
Pineapple, red – *Ananas bracteatus striatus*
Pineapple, ivory – *Ananas comosus* 'Variegatus'
Plantain lily – Hosta
Plume flower – *Celosia plumosa*
Poinsettia – *Euphorbia pulcherrima*
Polka dot plant – *Hypoestes sanguinolenta* (syn. *H.
  phyllostachya*)
Prayer plant – Maranta
Prickly pear – Opuntia
Pygmy date palm – *Phoenix roebelenii*
Queen's tears – *Billbergia nutans*
Rosary vine – *Ceropegia woodii*
Rose of China – *Hibiscus rosa-sinensis*
Rubber plant – *Ficus elastica*
Scarlet star – *Guzmania lingulata* (and hybrids)
Sensitive plant – *Mimosa pudica*
Sentry palm – *Howeia belmoreana* (syn. *Kentia
  belmoreana*)
Shrimp plant – *Beloperone guttata*
Slipper orchid – Cypripedium (syn.
  Paphiopedilum)
Snakeskin plant – Fittonia
Spanish moss – *Tillandsia usneoides*
Spathe flower – Spathiphyllum
Spider lily – *Hymenocallis x festalis*
Spider plant – *Chlorophytum comosum*
Spiraea, perennial – Astilbe
Spotted laurel – *Aucuba japonica*
Stag's horn fern – *Platycerium bifurcatum*
Star of Bethelehem – *Campanula isophylla*
Stove fern – *Pteris cretica*
Strawberry geranium – *Saxifraga stolonifera* (syn.
  S. sarmentosa)
String of hearts – *Ceropegia woodii*
Sundew – *Drosera capensis*
Swedish ivy – *Plectanthus oertendahlii*
Sweetheart plant – *Philodendron scandens*
Swiss cheese plant – *Monstera deliciosa*
Sword fern – *Nephrolepis exaltata*
Table fern – *Pteris cretica*
Umbrella plant – *Schefflera actinophylla*
Urn plant – *Aechmea fasciata*
Velvet plant – Gynura
Venus fly trap – *Dionaea muscipula*
Voodoo lily – *Sauromatum venosum*
  (syn. *S. guttatum*)
Wandering Jew – Tradescantia,
  Zebrina
Wax flower – Hoya, *Stephanotis
  floribunda*
Weeping fig – *Ficus benjamina*
Winter cherry – *Solanum
  capsicastrum, S. pseudocapsicum*
Zebra plant – *Aphelandra
  squarrosa, Calathea zebrina*

Index

Acknowledgements and credits

The publishers would like to thank the following for their generous help in the production of this book: Andrew J Smith, Manor Nurseries, Stockbridge Road, Timsbury, Hants, for providing plants, a location and their time for much of the step-by-step photography; Sean Flynn, The Garden Studio, 146 Columbia Road, London E2, for kindly lending a range of plant containers and equipment featured in the final chapter; Peter Watkins, Lease-a-Plant Ltd, M.K.M. Nurseries, Bulls Lane, Bell Bar, Herts, for providing plants for photography; The Dutch Nursery, Bell Bar, Brookmans Park, Herts, for providing plants for photography; The Camden Garden Centre, 2 Barker Drive, St Pancras Way, London NW1, for lending plants for photography; and The Chelsea Gardener, 125 Sydney Street, Kings Road, London SW3 for providing plants and containers for photography.

Special thanks are due to Stephanie Donaldson, who created and styled the plant displays featured in the final chapter; thanks also to Ann Venn, Nicky Walton and Diane Redfern for kindly opening up their homes to provide the settings for these plant displays.

All photography by John Freeman, with additional photographs, as follows, by Peter McHoy:

Key: t = top; b = bottom; l = left; c = centre; r = right.

Pages: 20 b, 23 t, 24 t, 26 b, 27 tl br, 28 b, 29 tl tc tr b, 30 t, 31 b, 32 t b, 33 t c bl br, 39 t, 46, 47 cr br, 58, 59, 63 b, 64, 70 br, 71, 73 cl cr bl br, 80 tr bc, 81 tl tc bl, 82 b, 83 tr, 84 bl br, 85 tl tr bl, 99 bl, 100, 101 tr, 103 tl bl br, 104, 112 b, 113 b.

NOTES

NOTES

NOTES

NOTES